A SOLDIER ON THE SOUTHERN FRONT

A SOLDIER ON THE SOUTHERN FRONT

The Classic Italian Memoir of World War I

EMILIO LUSSU

Translated from the Italian by Gregory Conti

Rizzoli
ex libris

J'ai plus de souvenirs que si j'avais mille ans.

BAUDELAIRE

Published in the United States of America in 2014
By Rizzoli Ex Libris, an imprint of
Rizzoli International Publications, Inc.
300 Park Avenue South
New York, NY 10010
www.rizzoliusa.com

Book design by Tina Henderson

2014 2015 2016 2017 / 10 9 8 7 6 5 4 3 2 1

Distributed in the U.S. trade by Random House, New York
Printed in U.S.A.

ISBN-13: 978-0-8478-4278-0
Library of Congress Catalog Control Number: 2013943440

AUTHOR'S NOTE

I wrote *A Soldier on the Southern Front* between 1936 and 1937 in a sanatorium in Clavadel, near Davos. I had retired there following the deterioration of the lung disease I had contracted in prison, which I had been unable to treat during my confinement on the island of Lipari and, after my escape, had neglected in France. Having finally decided to get well, I underwent a rather arduous operation and my convalescence forced me into a long period of inactivity. But even so, I never would have written the book without the insistence of Gaetano Salvemini.[1] Ever since 1921, following our mutual re-evocations of the war, he had been urging me to write a book—"the book," he called it in his letters. In exile, "the book" had become a sort of promissory note for the debt I owed him. At some point, pursuing an idea I had had in mind ever since I had read Federico Chabod's *On The Prince by Niccolò Machiavelli,* I came up with the presumptuous notion of writing something about *The Prince.* The day I brought it up with Salvemini, our friendship threatened to come crashing down. It was "the book" he was demanding from me, not some idle reflection about the Florentine secretary. So that's how my book on the war came to see the light. I sent the manuscript to Salvemini, who was in London, at the end of May 1937, and he responded with a several-hundred-word telegram. My friend was placated.

The first Italian edition was published in Paris by Edizioni Italiane di Cultura in early 1938, the second in Italy by Einaudi in 1945, after the liberation. On re-reading this testimony of the war, which I have left unchanged from its original version, I am reminded of Salvemini. And it is to him that I dedicate this edition.

Emilio Lussu
Rome, September 1960

The reader will not find in this book either a novel or a history. These are my personal recollections, put in order as best as I could, and limited to one year of the four years of war in which I took part. I haven't recounted anything except what I saw and what struck me most. I have not relied on my imagination but on my memory; and my comrades-in-arms, sometimes by way of some slightly changed names, will easily recognize both men and events. I have also stripped myself of my subsequent experience and have evoked the war as we actually lived it, with the thoughts and feelings we had at the time. This is not, therefore, a work with a thesis: It is intended merely as the account of an Italian witness to the Great War. In Italy, unlike France, Germany, and England, there are no books about the war. And this one, too, would never have been written but for a period of imposed rest.

Clavadel–Davos, April 1937

TRANSLATOR'S NOTE

For readers coming to Lussu's account of his experience on the southern front of World War I nearly a century after the events he describes, it may be helpful to have a brief outline of the military organization and chain of command in which he served.

When Italy entered the war in May of 1915 its land forces were composed of four armies, each commanded by a general, under the Supreme Command of General Luigi Cadorna. The four armies were made up of several corps, each commanded by a lieutenant general and were in turn composed of several divisions, each commanded by a major general. The remaining levels of command, in descending order, were brigades (brigadier general), regiments (colonel), companies (major or captain), platoons (lieutenant, second lieutenant), and squads (corporal).

Lussu began the war as a lieutenant in the Sassari Brigade, founded on March 1, 1915. Unlike all other Italian infantry brigades, the Sassari was recruited locally on the island of Sardinia, and most of the officers, like Lussu, came from the island. In 1916 the Sassari was under the command of the 3rd Army, commanded by a member of the Savoy dynasty, Italy's royal family, Prince Emanuele Filiberto of Savoy, Duke of Aosta. The brigade had a total strength of approximately 6,000 men, divided into two regiments of three battalions each.

The Sassari saw its first combat in the summer of 1915 in the First Battle of the Isonzo and distinguished itself in the Second Battle of the Isonzo. In May 1916, the start of the year recounted in the book, the brigade was sent to the Asiago Plateau to help in the Italian effort to stop the Austrian spring offensive. By the end of the war, the Sassari was the most highly decorated unit in the Italian army, its soldiers having earned 6 Military Orders of Savoy, 9 Gold Medals, 405 Silver Medals, and 551 Bronze Medals for Military Valor. Four of those medals were awarded to Emilio Lussu.

I

In late May 1916, my brigade—the 399th and 400th Regiments[2]—was still on the Carso.[3] It had been fighting solely on that front since the beginning of the war. By now we couldn't stand it anymore. Every square foot of terrain reminded us of a battle or the grave of a fallen comrade. We'd done nothing but take trenches and trenches and more trenches. After the trench of the "red cats" came the trench of the "black cats," and then it was the trench of the "green cats." But the situation never changed. As soon as we took one trench we had to take another. Trieste was still there, perched on the edge of the gulf, just as far away as ever, looming wearily. Our artillery hadn't fired on it even once. The Duke of Aosta, commander of our Third Army, invoked its name in all his daily orders and speeches to fire up the soldiers.

The prince didn't have much military acumen but he did have a great literary passion. He and his chief of staff made a perfect team. One wrote the speeches and the other delivered them. The duke learned them by heart and recited them in the oratorical style of an ancient Roman, with impeccable diction.

All the grand ceremonies, and they were rather frequent, were especially designed to highlight these performances. Unfortunately, the chief of staff wasn't a writer. So despite his best efforts, the general's memory in reciting the speeches won more of our army's esteem than the talent of his chief of staff in writing them. The general had a good voice, too. Apart from that, he was pretty unpopular.

One May afternoon, word reached us that, as a reward for all the sacrifices the brigade had endured, the duke had ordered that we be sent back behind the front line for several months' rest. And since this news was followed by an order that we prepare to be replaced by another brigade, we were convinced it was true. The soldiers welcomed the news with cheers and shouts of praise for the duke. They finally realized that there was some advantage in having a prince of the royal family as their army's commander. Only he could have granted such a long rest, and so far from the front line. Up to that time, their rest periods had been spent just a few kilometers from the trenches, under fire from enemy artillery. The division commander's cook had told our colonel's orderly (and the rumor had spread like lightning) that the duke wanted us to spend this rest period in a city. For the first time in the entire war his popularity was on the rise. The nicest things were said about him, and the news that he had had a heated argument with General Cadorna, in defense of our brigade, was deemed credible and made the rounds of all the units.

Our replacements arrived and that same night we headed down to the plains. After two days march we came to Aiello, a small town not far from what used to be the border.

We were overjoyed. Finally, we could live! Our heads were bursting with plans! After Aiello, we'd move on to a big city. Maybe Udine, who knew?

When we entered Aiello it was time for first rations. My battalion, the 3rd, was marching at the head of the line, with the 12th Company in the lead. The commander of the 12th was a cavalry officer, Reserve Lieutenant Grisoni. He had served as orderly officer for our brigade commander. When the commander died after being wounded by a grenade, Grisoni decided to stay in the brigade and came to serve in my battalion. As a cavalry officer he couldn't be assigned to an infantry unit, but the commanding general of the cavalry had given him special authorization, with the right to keep his ordnance and horse. The whole brigade knew who he was. On August 21, 1915, with forty volunteers, he had launched a sneak attack and taken a solidly dug-in enemy advance trench defended by a Hungarian battalion. The attack was an example of extreme bravery. But it was a different escapade that made him famous. One night, during one of our rest periods, after mixing together and drinking, without excessive moderation, a number of Piedmontese wines, he rode his horse with his customary stealth and daring into the officers' mess, where the colonel was eating with the officers from the regimental command. He didn't utter a single word, but his horse, which appeared to have a perfect knowledge of military hierarchy, proceeded to whinny and prance around the colonel for the longest time. This deed, received somewhat differently than the first, nearly got him sent back to the cavalry.

My battalion was filing by now, in march step, in the square in front of the town hall. There to watch them were the brigade commander, the regiment commander, and the civic authorities. The lead company, four to a row, went marching by in martial fashion. The soldiers were muddy, but their trench getup made the parade more solemn. When they arrived opposite the authorities, Lieutenant Grisoni stood up in his stirrups, turned to the company, and shouted, "Eyes left!"

It was their salute to the brigade commander.

But it was also the agreed-upon signal for the company's 1st Platoon to spring into action. Immediately, a carefully orchestrated fanfare shattered the ceremonial protocol. A trumpet, made out of a big metal coffee pot, blared the call to attention, followed by a motley assembly of instruments sounding their agreement, all of them improvised, with the largest portion made up of those that could make a loud noise to accompany the beat. Mess tin lids turned into cymbals. Old canvas baggage tarps were ingeniously adapted into drums. Pistons, clarions, and flutes were arranged out of closed fists blown into by specialists who, opening first one finger and then another, managed to toot to their hearts' content. The end result was an admirable musical blend of the merriment of war.

The brigade commander wrinkled his brow, but in the end he smiled.

A reasonable man, he didn't find it improper that soldiers, having lived in the mud and under fire for the better part of a year, should allow themselves a frolic, even if it was not in line with regulations.

Following the parade, the whole regiment moved into quarters in Aiello. Later that afternoon the mayor invited all the officers back to the town hall to enjoy a glass of wine and a speech. In a trembling voice, he read:

"It is a great honor for me, et cetera, et cetera. In the glorious war that the Italian people are fighting under the ingenious and heroic command of His Majesty the King . . ."

On the word "king," we all snapped to attention, as we were required to do, with a loud and simultaneous clacking of heels and spurs. The sudden blast of that military salute reverberated in the municipal great hall like a gunshot. The mayor, a profane civilian, couldn't have imagined that his modest reference to the sovereign would provoke such a clamorous demonstration of constitutional loyalty. He was a distinguished gentleman and, with forewarning, he certainly would not have failed to appreciate, in the appropriate measure and degree, such a patriotic act. But taken in this way, completely unawares, he flinched and made a slight jump that raised him several centimeters above his normal height. All the color drained out of his face. He turned his uncertain gaze toward the group of motionless officers and waited. The sheet of paper with the words of his speech written on it had dropped out of his hands and was lying, like a culprit, at his feet.

The colonel was wearing an honest smile of self-satisfaction, pleased to see highlighted, albeit only temporarily, the superiority of the military authorities over the civilian. With an expression of contained pride, which anyone without a long experience of military command would struggle futilely to display, he turned his gaze from the mayor to us and from us to the mayor, and, with that morsel of malice that insinuates itself into the heart of even the meekest of men, he realized how he could intimidate the mayor even more. He barked, "Officers, long live the king!"

"Long live the king!" we echoed, shouting out the phrase as a monosyllable.

Contrary to the colonel's expectation, the mayor didn't bat an eyelash and shouted along with us.

The mayor was a man of the world. Back in control of himself by now, he picked up the paper off the floor, and resumed his speech.

"We shall win, because it is written so in the book of fate . . ."

Where that book was, surely none of us, including the mayor, actually knew. And even less so, what might have been written in that irretrievably lost book. In any event, the phrase did not provoke any special reaction. On the other hand, there was remarkable attention for this other passage:

"War is not as hard as we imagine it to be. This morning when I saw your soldiers coming into the city in celebration, accompanied by the sound of that fanfare more joyous than one could ever conceive, I understood, and the entire population understood along with me, that war has its own beautiful attractions . . ."

The cavalry lieutenant saluted, rattling his spurs, as though the compliment had been directed especially to him. The mayor continued.

"Beautiful and sublime attractions. Unhappy is he who cannot feel them! Because, oh gentlemen, it is beautiful indeed to die for your country . . ."

This allusion didn't appeal to anyone, not even the colonel. The judgment was a classic, but the mayor was not the most suitable person to make us appreciate, literarily, the beauty of death, even such a glorious one. Even the demeanor with which the mayor had accompanied his exclamation had been inappropriate. It seemed as though he'd wanted to say, "You are more beautiful dead than alive." A sizable portion of the officers coughed and looked at the mayor disdainfully. The cavalry lieutenant displayed his restlessness with a rattling of spurs.

Did the mayor understand how we felt? Probably, because he hurried to conclude, praising the king. He said precisely this:

"Long live our glorious king, scion of a warrior race!"

The cavalry lieutenant was the closest to a large table covered with cups of sparkling wine. Quickly, he grabbed one that was still full, raised it, and cried out, "Long live the king of cups!"

For the colonel it was a direct blow to the chest. He looked at the lieutenant, amazed, as though he couldn't believe his eyes and ears. He looked at the officers, appealing to them as witnesses, and said, more disconsolate than severe, "Lieutenant Grisoni, again today you have had too much to drink. Kindly leave the room and wait for my orders."

The lieutenant clicked his spurs, stiffened to attention, took one step back, and saluted.

"Yes, sir!"

And he walked out, his whip tucked under his arm, visibly satisfied.

II

The chorus leader intoned:

"That little bunch of flowers . . ."

The company chorus answered:

"That comes from the mountains . . ."[4]

And the song brought the weary soldiers back to life. We had been marching for three days. The immobility of our long sedentary stay on the Carso had left us all incapable of strenuous effort. The march was painful for everyone. Our only comfort was the thought that we were going to the mountains.

Our rest in Aiello hadn't lasted more than a week. The Austrians had unleashed their great offensive, between Mount Pasubio and the Val Lagarina. Breaking through our lines at Peak XII, they were now looking down on the high plateau of Asiago.[5] The brigade, leaving behind its temporary quarters, had crossed the plains of the Veneto by train. Now, at forced march, it was approaching the slopes of the high plateau.

The chorus was growing more lively, but each of the men was lost in his own thoughts. Life in the trenches was over. Now, they had told us, we would be counterattacking, maneuvering. And in the mountains. Finally! Among ourselves, we had always talked about the war in the mountains as though it were some kind of privileged rest. So now we too would be seeing trees, forests and springs, valleys and blind spots that would make us forget, along with our up-in-smoke rest period, that horrible rock pile of the Carso—barren, without a blade of grass or a drop of water, all the same, always the same, no shelter, apart from the occasional sinkhole: magnets for volleys of high-caliber artillery fire, which everything fell into helter-skelter, men and mules, the living and the dead. We would finally be able, in our hours of idleness, to lie out in the sun, or sleep under a tree, without being seen, without being awakened by a bullet in the leg. And from the mountaintops we would have, stretching out before us, a horizon and a view in place of the interminable walls of the trenches and the barbed-wire entanglements. And we would finally be liberated from that miserable life, lived fifty or a hundred yards from the enemy trenches, in that ferocious promiscuity, in a constant series of bayonet assaults to the tune of hand grenades and rifle shots fired at loopholes.[6] We would stop killing each other, every day, without hate. The war of maneuver would be something else. A successful maneuver, two hundred thousand, three hundred thousand prisoners, just like that, in a single day, without that horrific, generalized slaughter; just the success of an ingenious strategic encirclement. And who knows, maybe we'd actually be able to win and be done with the war for good.

The only shortcoming of the war of maneuver was that you had to march; all the time march.

A cavalry regiment crossed the road in front of us and we had to stop to let it file by. Lucky them, up on their horses! But we soon realized that they, too, were dead tired.

"The gentlemens' way to go to war," the foot soldiers shouted up to the lancers, hunched over in their saddles.

"Lucky you," they responded, "you get to walk on your own two feet. Us, we're always on horseback, always on horseback. Not able to march on our own legs! Having to work for yourself and then for your horse. What a life!"

When the cavalry were gone, the company took up the chorus again.

Now the road was filling up with refugees. There wasn't a living soul left on the Asiago plateau. The population of the Seven Communes was pouring down onto the plains in disarray, dragging along on their oxcarts and mules, old people, women, and children, and what little furniture they'd been able to salvage from their homes so hurriedly abandoned to the enemy. The farmers driven off their land were like shipwreck survivors. Nobody was crying, but their faces were blank. This was the convoy of pain. The carts, creeping along, seemed like a funeral cortege.

Our column stopped its singing and fell silent. You couldn't hear anything else there on the road but our march step and the creaking of the cart wheels. This was a new spectacle for us. On the Carso front, it was we who were the invaders, and the farmers who had abandoned their homes ahead of our advance were Slavs. But we hadn't seen them.

A cart went by, longer than the others. Its two straw

mattresses were occupied by an old woman, a young mother, and two children. An old farmer, sitting in front, his legs dangling, was steering the oxen. He stopped the oxen and asked a soldier for some tobacco for his pipe.

"Smoke it, grandpa!" the corporal at the head of the line shouted at him and, without stopping, filled his hands with all the tobacco he had.

The soldiers followed suit. The old man, his hands overflowing with packets and cigars, looked in surprise at all that wealth. The column kept on marching in silence. As though an order had been issued to everyone, they all threw their tobacco onto the cart. The old man asked, "And what are you going to smoke now, boys?"

His question broke the silence. By way of response, someone intoned a lighthearted song from the marching repertory, and the column followed in chorus.

I kept my eyes on the guy next to me, "Uncle Francesco." He was the oldest soldier in the company; he'd also fought in the Libyan war back in 1911. The men called him Uncle Francesco because, besides being the oldest, he was also the father of five children. He was marching in step, to the rhythm of the chorus, and, like everybody else, he was singing out loud. His footsteps were heavy under the weight of his backpack. There was no expression of joy on his face. The cheerful words of the song came out of his mouth like strangers. Uncle Francesco was one thing, his song was another. His head bowed, his eyes staring at the ground, he was a long way off from the march and from his comrades.

"Open ranks!" some of the men shouted from the middle of the company. "The colonel's coming through!"

I turned to look back. The colonel, on horseback, followed by his adjutant, was coming through the middle of the column. We were already marching in open ranks to make room for the column of refugees; there wasn't much free space left on the road. We moved further toward the side of the road, but the colonel was still forced to keep our pace to avoid bumping into soldiers or against the carts with his horse. When he reached me, he told me he was pleased to see the men so cheerful and gave me twenty lire to divide up among the singers. As he was moving away, he noticed Uncle Francesco. His age, voice, and posture had caught his attention. He asked me who he was. I answered that he was a farmer from the south and added a few details.

"Good soldier?" the colonel asked.

"Excellent," I replied.

"Here's another five lire, for him, just for him."

Uncle Francesco realized that we were talking about him. He looked up and kept marching and singing without losing his composure. The colonel gave him a pat on the back and went off. News of the donation spread instantly and the chorus grew more lively.

"Oh fisherman of London . . ." the chorus leader sang.

"Blondie, my beautiful blonde," the chorus responded.

Uncle Francesco kept on singing, his head bowed and his voice strong. The farmers looked at us from their oxcarts, impassive. The cart wheels scraped against the gravel, emitting a plaintive accompaniment to the cheerful chorus.

We reached our day's destination just before sundown.

The day was still warm. Outside their tents, the men were lying on the grass, resting. The weariest, their hands clasped behind their heads, stretched out and motionless, were looking up at the sky in flames. Others were chatting, their voices low. Somebody was signing lullabies from his hometown. The only things moving were the sentinels on the perimeter of the camp.

The small groups sprang to life when an NCO came back from the supply wagon with some wine flasks and tobacco. He had spent the whole twenty lire. In war you don't think about tomorrow. Soon the flasks were passing from hand to hand and the voices were getting louder.

"To the colonel's health!"

"To the colonel's health!"

Just one young voice split off from the others, hostile. "To the health of that whore, his mother!"

His comrades protested.

"Hey, what do you want, that instead of the wine the colonel should stick a couple of rounds in your belly?"

Unnoticed, I looked on at the scene. The soldier didn't answer; he stayed there stretched out on the grass and didn't drink. I picked him out right away and recognized him. He surely had never had anything to do with the colonel.

Gradually, the voices died down. Now Uncle Francesco was talking. Serious, like a patriarch. The others listened to him, smoking.

"Never in my life have I earned five lire all at once. Never earned five lire, not even in a week. Except during the haying season, mowing with a scythe, from the first light of dawn until twilight.

I walked off. It was time for the officers' mess.

III

On the edge of the Asiago plateau, at thirty-five hundred feet, it was pure chaos. We'd arrived there on June 5 via Val Frenzela from Valstagna, under the tightest security measures, because it wasn't clear where our guys were and where the Austrians were. The regiment deployed between the hilltops around Stoccaredo and the Gallio–Foza road, and my battalion took up a position at Buso, a tiny village at the head of the Val Frenzela. Our advance posts were sprinkled about down in the basin, toward Ronchi, along the routes that could have been used by the vanguard of an enemy attack. All we knew was that they had crossed the Val d'Assa and taken Asiago, and were fanning out in our direction, on this side of Gallio. I was told that, somewhere between us and them, there were still some lost Italian units. What was certain was that the enemy was boldly taking advantage of their success: In the basins around Asiago, a number of field artillery batteries were moving around in plain sight. The bridge across Val d'Assa, destroyed by our side, had been rebuilt by the Austrians in a few days. All our artillery had fallen into enemy hands. We didn't have any more on the entire high plateau, not one piece.

Only Fort Lisser, an old fort dismantled in 1915, fired its two 149-caliber guns, and always on our troops. Fortunately, most of the rounds didn't explode, and we didn't take any casualties. A few days later the fort was dubbed, by our war correspondents, the "Lion of the High Plateau."

The battalion commander sent me, with a platoon, in the direction of Stoccaredo. My orders were to make contact with one of our army units that was supposed to be down there and get them to give me information about the enemy. Worried that we might be captured by the Austrians, I'd asked to take the whole company with me; the major didn't want to give me any more than a squad. In the end we settled on a compromise and I was given a platoon.

The sun had already gone down when, just north of Stoccaredo, I ran into a battalion of the 301st Infantry. It was under the command of a lieutenant colonel, fifty or so, who I found out in the open, sitting at a makeshift table made out of tree limbs, a bottle of brandy in hand. He greeted me very warmly and offered me a glass of brandy.

"Thanks," I said. "I don't drink liquor."

"You don't drink liquor?" the lieutenant colonel asked me, concerned.

He pulled a notebook out of the pocket of his battle jacket and wrote, "Met a lieutenant who didn't drink liquor. June 5, 1916."

He had me repeat my name, which I had already told him when I introduced myself, and he added it to the note. So as not to waste time, I told him right away what my orders were that had brought me all that way to see him. But before he would answer me, he wanted to know some details about my life and my studies. So he learned that I was a reserve officer who had left university when the war broke out. But it was still the liquor question that struck him most.

"Do you perhaps belong to some religious sect?" he asked.

"No," I replied, laughing. "Why would you think that?"

"Strange, extremely strange. And wine, do you drink wine?"

"A little at table, you know, a little during meals."

I repeated my questions about the enemy positions and ours. But he was in no hurry. He drank another brandy, and then he accompanied me, strolling slowly, to an observation post about fifty meters away, holding on all the while to his bottle and glass—out of habit, certainly, because at the observation post he never took a drink.

The observation post still had a clear view, illuminated by the last rays of sunlight: On the horizon to the north, about thirty kilometers as the crow flies, Peak XII. Opposite, the range of mountains ending at Mount Zebio, the crests of Gallio, and standing over all the others, further to the right, Mount Fior. Between us and those peaks, the Asiago basin. Further down, right underneath us, the smaller Ronchi basin.

"Where are the Austrians?" I asked.

"Ah, that I don't know. That's something nobody knows. They're in front of us. They could, from one minute to the next, be behind us. That depends on the circumstances. What's certain is that they're all over the place, and that, other than my battalion, there are no other Italian troops."

I asked for clarification on the position of the highest mountain, which he had told me was Mount Fior.

"Our guys are there. That's certain. The Austrians haven't reached there yet. The mountain is two thousand meters high. That's why our command calls it the 'Key to the High Plateau.'"

The lieutenant colonel used the bottle to point out the various positions. Frequently, he tilted the bottle over the glass as though he wanted to fill it, but, on each occasion, he stopped the bottle in time, and the glass stayed empty.

"In order not to lose it, our command has amassed at least twenty battalions on that 'key,' while here, at the 'door'" counting everybody, we're no more than a handful. The whole idea is wrong from the start. But it says in the textbooks that by holding the top of a mountain, you can keep the enemy from passing through the underlying valley. You see, down there, the mouth of the Val Frenzela, right underneath us? From the mouth to Mount Fior it's no farther than four or five kilometers as the crow flies. If the Austrians force their way through the mouth, through the door, they can get a whole army through without taking a single casualty, while the key sits up there, hanging on the wall. You don't drink, eh? You don't drink!"

"It seems to me that if we have twenty battalions up there, the Austrians can't pass through here."

"And, from up there, how do our twenty battalions stop them? With artillery? But we don't have a single piece, and there won't ever be any up there because there aren't any roads. With machine guns and rifles? Useless weapons at that distance. And so? So nothing. Just because if we happen to be imbeciles, that doesn't mean that the commanders on the other side are any smarter than us. The art of war is the same for everybody. You'll see, the Austrians will attack Mount Fior with forty battalions, and it'll be useless. And we're even. That's the military art."

I found the conversation interesting, but night was coming on and I didn't want to go back in the dark. I had opened a topographical map and was trying my best to orient it correctly.

"You don't drink!" he said again. Then, in a mocking tone, "Don't trust the maps. Otherwise you'll never find your regiment again. Take it from me, a veteran career officer. I fought in the whole Africa campaign. We lost Adwa because we had some maps. That's why we ended up going west instead of going east. A little like attacking Venice instead of attacking Verona. In the mountains, maps are only intelligible to people who already know the region, because they were born and raised there. But people who already know the terrain don't need maps."

Leaving the observation post behind, we made our way back to his battalion command. He went over to the tree-limb table, sat down, and drank two glasses of brandy, one to my health and one to his. I thanked him, and, putting myself at the head of the platoon that was waiting for me, got back on the road to rejoin the regiment.

There must have been something to the lieutenant colonel's theories. That evening, I got lost on the way back. That wouldn't have happened if I had gone back the same way we had come. But it was already late and I was looking for a shortcut in order to avoid the road going to Buso, which was too long. The path I'd chosen ran through the woods. A few meters from an intersection, on a piece of uneven terrain covered with bushes and shrubs, we were greeted by a volley of rifle fire. I realized too late that we had veered off to the left instead of going right, toward Val Frenzela.

"Hit the dirt!" I cried. "Move right, and spread out!"

The platoon dropped to the ground, and started spreading out, moving on all fours. We were under fire but protected by the lay of the land and the thick woods. The shrubs hid us completely.

"Damn Hungarians!" the sergeant beside me swore. "They put a hole in my arm."

"Hungarians?" I murmured.

"Yes, sir, lieutenant. I managed to get a glimpse of one of them standing up. He's got a four-leaf clover on his pants."

"No," I said. "You're wrong. They're Bosnians."

They'd told us, in fact, at division headquarters, that the enemy advance guard was formed by a Bosnian division. The Bosnian uniforms didn't have a four-leaf clover.

The platoon was spread out and calmly firing away. The sergeant was wrapping his wounded arm, helped by a soldier. The superiority of the troops we were facing was evident. The incoming fire was from a company at least. If they had attacked us we would have been overwhelmed. I ordered bayonets on and spread the word to stay elbow to elbow, ready to counterattack.

Meanwhile I was worried. I had been given orders to do a reconnaissance and make contact with our left flank to get clarification on the situation, not to get myself involved in combat. The platoon was an escort, to guard against being surprised by patrols, not a unit capable of withstanding a fight like this. So I decided to fall back.

After the initial flare-up, the enemy fire died down. Now they were firing only isolated shots. To cover the noise of our retreat, I had a hand grenade set off. The soldier closest to me lit a pineapple-shaped *Sipe*, calmly checked that the fuse was lit, held it for a few seconds, jumped straight up on his feet, and threw it in a high arc so it wouldn't be blocked by the trees.[7] The bomb exploded nicely, on its way down, with a blast that the forest made even bleaker. The fragments scattered with strident hissing sounds, cats meowing. It was the first hand grenade we'd exploded on the high plateau. It was followed by a moment of silence in the woods. From the enemy lines, a sonorous voice responded, in Italian, "In your face!"

The rifle fire started up again, more intense. In front of us, a flare shot up into the air, way high, lighting up the woods and the entire Ronchi valley. We flattened on the ground like leaves.

"Maybe the sergeant is right," I thought. "They must be Hungarians from the Adriatic coast. The Bosnians certainly don't speak Italian."

The platoon's retreat was carried out in squads, moving back in stages, slowly, so we wouldn't lose contact with each other. By now it was pitch dark and it was hard to maneuver while maintaining a modicum of order.

It took us more than an hour before, no longer under fire, we could all come together, safe again. The last to complete the move was the 4th Squad. They had taken a prisoner. Under the light of the flare, a lone soldier, between us and the enemy, had come walking toward us with his hands in the air. The squad saw him and, when the flare went out, they captured him. A prisoner was just what we needed to get information about the enemy. I was really pleased. I said to the 4th Squad's corporal, "I'll make sure your squad gets a reward."

The prisoner, unarmed, was surrounded by the squad, two soldiers holding him by his arms. Nobody was talking, neither the prisoner nor the others. Each of them was convinced of the uselessness of a conversation held in a foreign language. But even so, in the dark and the silence, that atmosphere of fellow feeling that is always created in such circumstances was immediately established. The victors want to lavish on the vanquished some authentication of their goodness; the vanquished accept it so as not to seem contemptuous. The prisoner was eating the chocolate the soldiers had offered him, and when I consented, because we were under cover, he lit up the cigarette he had been given. I ordered roll call to be sure no one had been left behind, wounded or missing, and turned on the flashlight I had in my pocket.

"But he's from our regiment!" exclaimed the sergeant who was checking the bandage on his arm and had moved between me and the prisoner.

"Who is from our regiment?" I asked, distracted.

"The prisoner."

"Damn, damn, damn!" murmured the 4th Squad's corporal, between his teeth.

The flashlight was shining on the prisoner's face. Shocked, his pupils dilated, he too was looking all around. The cigarette fell out of his mouth. The uniform was ours. On his beret, the number 399, our regiment. The badges, those of our brigade. On his epaulets, the number of his company, the 9th. And the same battalion as ours.

"What's your name?" I asked him.

"Marrasi, Giuseppe," he told me, dejected.

I asked the names of his company and platoon commanders and he told me. They were the names of my colleagues from the battalion.

"How is it you ended up like this, mixed up with us?"

"I got lost."

"Was it Ninth Company that was firing on us?"

"Yes, sir."

When the roll had been called we headed out again. The soldier from the 9th was talking with his comrades.

"So something went wrong, huh?"

"You figured you were done with the war, you son of a bitch! Admit it, you would have given one of your eyes for us to turn out to be Austrians."

Marrasi protested, "No, but no, I'm telling you . . ."

"Some stomach you've got! You wolfed down that chocolate like a real Austrian. You owe me . . ."

IV

The battalion stayed put for four days, between Buso and the Gallio–Foza road, in contact with the enemy advance posts. The Austrians, having stopped at the mouth of Val Frenzela, were concentrating all their forces against Mount Fior. It was defended mainly by groups of Alpini battalions: the Val Maira, the Seven Communes, and the Bassano, and some others whose names I've forgotten.[8] They were all regional battalions, recruited in the upper Veneto, so they were all fighting near their own homes. There was also an infantry regiment and a few other detached battalions. The 1st and 2nd Battalions of our regiment had also been sent there as an emergency measure. My battalion, once we were replaced by other units that had come up through the Val Frenzela, was the last to join them. The battalion adjutant major had been gravely wounded and I, who up to that time had been commanding the 10th Company, was named adjutant of the 3rd Battalion.

We set off just after midnight from Foza. The brigade commander came to see us off. He would shortly be joining us, too. He had a son fighting in the Alpini battalions.

We climbed up the rocky face of the mountain single file, on a mule trail. We were out of earshot of the fighting on Mount Fior. The wind carried it off to our left, toward Val d'Assa. The silence of the night was broken only by our footsteps and the metal tips of our walking sticks. From time to time, faintly, we could see the flash of a rocket. To our right, in the distance, beyond the opposite slope of Mount Tonderecar, we could hear the frequent cries of a fox, shrill and raucous, like a sarcastic laugh.

The serpentine mule trail ended at Malga Lora, a grassy, treeless basin that opened up under the peaks of Mount Fior.[9] The pinnacles on the rim of the basin are the continuation of the mountain slopes, gradually descending to Mount Tonderecar. The head of the battalion arrived there at the first light of dawn, when a column of wounded, treated at the first-aid post in the Malga and carried on stretchers, was starting its descent. The basin opened up before us, green and restful, like an oasis. There were still some small remnants of snow around the bushes and between the rocks. The major decided to stop there to get the battalion back into formation.

By now the sound of rifle fire was quite distinct. The top of Mount Fior was no more than a few hundred meters from us. We were too close to it to be able to see it. But the shots were isolated. The major had a big topographical map spread out on the ground and he was bent over it, smoking. Suddenly, we were raked by a burst of fire from two machine guns somewhere above us. The major left the map lying on the ground and raced over to the head of the battalion to order the men to move back. In no time, we moved out of range and scattered ourselves among the rocks.

After that first surprise, it didn't take us long to figure out that the enemy was in control of the mouth of the basin. Evidently, during the night they had taken one of the highest points on the mountain and placed their machine guns there. But all the positions on either side of them were still ours, otherwise nobody would have been able to stay in the Malga. But the Alpini groups' command and the sector command were still there, along with the first-aid post, where the wounded were coming from.

The column of wounded also had to stop and fall back.

"Take two orderlies," the major said to me, "go over to the command hut, and find out what happened during the night. Tell the Alpini command we're here and waiting for orders."

The major garnished his speech with profanity. He was Tuscan, from Florence, and cursed day and night. When he was agitated, he borrowed unstintingly from the entire repertory he'd learned on the banks of the Arno.

With the two orderlies, I made my way as fast as possible across the terrain being strafed by the machine guns, and in just a few minutes we found cover. We could see the Alpini groups' command at the other end of the pasture, its back against the slope. The red cross of the first-aid post was hoisted up alongside it, atop a log cabin, an old shelter for cows out to pasture in the summer. I headed toward it. The cabin and its surroundings were crowded with wounded waiting to be transported to Foza. A constant flow of more wounded was coming down from above. I asked for the commander of the groups. I was shown an officer who was standing beside the building, wrapped in a large ordnance cape, his gaze fixed on the heights of the pasture.

I introduced myself. He had a helmet on, and I couldn't make out his rank, but when he shook my hand the stripes on his jacket showed. He was a colonel. He listened to what I had to say, apparently calm, despite the insomnia I could see on his face and the alarming communications he was receiving from every part of the sector. Next to him, a captain kept on writing and didn't even look up.

"We're in bad shape and we don't have enough troops to hold out," he told me. "We have no artillery, except the guns at Fort Lisser, ten kilometers from here, which have killed one of my officers and some of my soldiers. We have no machine guns. The enemy artillery has knocked them all out of commission."

The colonel made a gesture of distress. From under his cape, he pulled out a white metal canteen, contemplated it, as though to make sure it was still the same one, and took a swig. Then he spoke again.

"Last night in the saddle we were attacked by superior forces. An entire company was wiped out. A company from your regiment, the Fourth. Not a single officer survived. They had replaced one of my battalions, which had been wiped out yesterday, in the afternoon. Inform your command."

"Yes, sir."

The colonel looked for his canteen again and took another drink.

"Tell your battalion commander that, staying clear of the terrain under fire from the machine guns, going further right, he should attack the saddle. Is your battalion tough?

"Tough as hell!"

"Ready for anything?"

"Anything."

The colonel, who still had his canteen in hand, offered me a drink.

"Tell your commander that you found me here, that you found Colonel Stringari here, commander of the Alpini groups, ready to die."

"Yes, sir."

"And you tell him that here we all have to die. All of us have to die. That's our duty. Tell him that. Understand?"

"Yes, sir."

I ran back down on the double to report to the major. When I told him we all had to die, the major erupted in profanity.

"We all have to die? He can start by dying himself. That's his business. He can go right ahead. For us, the problem is staying alive, not dying. What the hell, if we all die the Austrians will go all the way down to Bassano, smoking their pipes. So it's the saddle we're supposed to attack?"

"The saddle."

"Give me a drink," the major shouted to his orderly.

The orderly handed him his canteen of brandy.

Attacking the saddle was a difficult operation. But the major, despite his agitation, knew how to command the battalion. We might just pull it off.

The battalion had already closed ranks and all the companies were in order. The major sent Lieutenant Santini, from the 9th, to check out the terrain with his platoon. He was thinking we'd have to take a longer approach, so we'd have the advantage of attacking the saddle from above, from the right, rather than attacking it straight on, from below.

As the companies started moving out, a second lieutenant from the Alpini battalions arrived from Malga Lora carrying a written order. The colonel was ordering the battalion to suspend the action against the saddle, and as quickly as possible to take a position on Mount Spill, opposite Mount Fior. This amounted to a totally different operation, because the saddle was to the right of Malga Lora and Mount Spill to the left. The major asked for an explanation. The second lieutenant explained that the colonel was afraid that, any minute now, the Austrians might force their way through our positions on Mount Fior and push forward. Immediately following my talk with the colonel, the Bassano Battalion, down to forty men, had been forced to retreat. So we had to do something to reinforce our position at our most delicate point.

Right in front of the Alpini officer the major cursed the orders and counterorders. But he began shifting the battalion toward Mount Spill.

He was more agitated that day than normal. All he did, every other minute, was ask if the mule that was carrying the baggage of the battalion command had arrived yet. But the mule was nowhere to be seen. The baggage was of absolutely no use to us, and the major's impatience must have had another cause. It didn't take me long to realize that he was waiting for his personal bag, and not those of the command. There were only a few of us in the battalion who knew that he was used to wearing body armor when we were engaged in combat. So as not to weigh himself down during our march, he had left it behind with the baggage. It was certainly in his personal bag. He kept feeling his chest with both hands. But the armor wasn't there. He was accustomed to the risks of war; he had fought in the Libyan war too, probably without armor. But now, the armor had become an obsession that kept him in a permanent state of agitation. He showered the battalion with curses.

The battalion was climbing up Mount Spill, struggling. The terrain was rough and covered with bushes. Lieutenant Santini's platoon was still ahead of us, scouting. An enemy patrol, with a machine gun, fell into its hands. We couldn't figure out how the patrol had got through because, to our front, our lines were still holding. Probably it was a patrol from another sector that had gotten lost. Unable to understand the prisoners, we sent them to the rear. This time they really were Bosnians. This happy episode calmed the major down and he ordered that they all be given cigarettes and bread.

Around five in the afternoon, we reached the top of Mount Spill. Mount Fior was still holding out. Infantry battalions from other regiments had also arrived on Mount Spill. A second lieutenant in one of those battalions saw us arrive and came to meet us to set up our communications. When he went back up to his command, I decided to go with him so I could get a better idea of the forces our battalion could count on to our left. And, for the second time, I happened upon the lieutenant colonel from the observation post at Stoccaredo. He was now commanding two battalions of his regiment, the command of which, along with one battalion, had remained in Stoccaredo. He too was under the command of the Alpini groups.

He was stretched out on a field blanket under an open tent, protected by a big rock. It was he who saw me first and called out to me.

"Come here. Sit down for a minute. What did I tell you? Look at the Austrians attacking Mount Fior."

I sat down on the ground, near the tent. He remained lying down. A bottle, with no label, and a glass, were within arm's reach. He asked me again about my studies.

"Ah, you too know the University of Turin? Well, great! Let's have a little chat, no talking about war."

He was Piedmontese.

"War, always war! It's enough to make you crazy. May I speak frankly with you?"

"Certainly," I said. "I wouldn't have it otherwise."

"I'm an officer by mistake. Honestly, do I have the face of a career officer? I did two years of university, in letters. Always the first in my class. That was my career. But my father had this idea fixed in his head, stuck there like a nail. What am I saying, a nail? It was a sword. He forced me to go to the military academy. My father was a colonel, my grandfather a general, my great-grandfather a general, my great-great grandfather . . . I've got eight generations of officers in my blood, all in a direct line. They've ruined me."

The lieutenant colonel spoke slowly. He drank in small swigs, the way you sip a cup of coffee.

"I defend myself by drinking. Otherwise, I'd already be in the nuthouse. Against the hostility of the world, an honest man defends himself by drinking. It's more than a year now that I've been fighting in this war, on just about every front, and I've yet to look a single Austrian in the face. Yet we go on killing each other every day. Killing each other without even knowing each other, without even seeing each other! It's horrible! That's why we're all drunk all the time, on one side and the other. Have you ever killed anyone? You, personally, I mean, with your own hands?"

"I hope not."

"Me, nobody. I mean, not anyone I've seen. But if we all, by common agreement, a solemn promise, stopped drinking, maybe the war would end. But if the other side drinks, then I drink, too. You see, I've been around a long time. It's not the artillery that keeps us on our feet, we foot soldiers. On the contrary, quite often our own artillery pounds us into the ground, shelling us instead of the enemy."

"The Austrian artillery fires on its infantry all the time, too."

"Naturally. The technique is the same. Abolish the artillery on both sides and the war goes on. But try to abolish wine and liquor. Just try it. Try it."

"I've already tried it."

"An insignificant and deplorable personal matter. But

extend your example into an order, a general rule. None of us would ever move again. The soul of the combatant in this war, his fighting spirit, is alcohol. The war's main engine is alcohol. That's why the soldiers, in their infinite wisdom, call it gasoline."

The lieutenant colonel stood up. His pale face lit up with a smile. He pulled out a book from under a pile of papers. He shook it in front of my face and asked me, "What book is this? Guess. What book?"

"The manual of regulations for wartime service," I said without conviction, trying to read the title.

"Me, wartime service! You must be crazy. Come on, guess."

I figured it was a current book, related to his predilection. "*Bacchus in Tuscany*," I said.

"No, but that's close."

"*Anacreon*."

"No."

I tried to think of another illustrious drinker. The lieutenant colonel shoved the title page under my eyes. I read it: *The Art of Making Your Own Liquor*.

"You see what I mean," he explained. "With this damn mountain war we can't even carry two bottles with us. This way, I can make as much as I want. I know, there's a big difference between distilled alcohol and the powdered stuff. But this is better than nothing."

"A rare art," I said.

"Rare," the lieutenant colonel repeated. "Believe me, it's worth every bit as much as the art of war."

On Mount Fior the battle was raging.

V

"Why hasn't that gravedigger come up here yet?" the major was saying to me, irritated that the medical officer still hadn't joined the battalion. "If I don't teach him a good lesson, he'll end up setting up the first-aid post in his own house."

He was getting more and more agitated. The command baggage still hadn't arrived. And the battalion had been on Mount Spill for more than four hours now.

He really got furious when two carabinieri presented themselves at command, accompanying a soldier from 9th Company apprehended in Foza without being able to justify his absence from his unit. The brigade command had him brought to the front line, persuaded that he had been trying to desert.

"A deserter in my battalion!" cried the major. "My battalion has never had a deserter. But I'll have him shot at once!"

Unless those two carabinieri were Tuscan, they'd never heard as many curses in their lives as they heard in those few minutes.

The major interrogated the soldier. He was Giuseppe Marrasi, the "Bosnian." He claimed to have lost his haversack with the two reserve cans of meat. To avoid being punished, he had retraced his steps in the hope he'd be able to find it, near Foza, at the location of his company's last bivouac.

"What reserve and what bivouac!" the major shot back, and to the carabinieri, "Why haven't you shot him yet?"

The soldier was saved by the arrival of the driver and the mule loaded with the command baggage. The major suspended the interrogation, dismissed the carabinieri, and turned his attention to the bags. I left in order to save him any embarrassment, accompanied by Marrasi.

"You," I said to him, "are developing some bad habits. First you lose your haversack and then you lose yourself. What are you going to lose next?"

He didn't respond either to my observations or to my question.

The major reappeared, his chest puffed out, smiling. He looked reborn. He saw Marrasi and me and walked over to us.

"What's all this chatter about desertion those dumbbell carabinieri are trying to give me? If there are any deserters around here it's them, hiding out behind the lines. Marrasi, get to your company! And I don't want to hear any crap about the cans of meat. Buy them, steal them, but the cans have to be where they're supposed to be. Understood?"

"Yes, sir."

"Get back to your company and that's the last I want to hear about it."

Just before midnight, the battalion received the order to go to the front line, on Mount Fior, with all four of its companies, the pioneers, and the machine-gun section. We took up our position in the dark, a bit helter-skelter, occupying the space that the other troops, farther to the right, had left us. We spent the whole night digging.

We were in a tough situation. We realized it at dawn, when the Austrians opened fire. In the order that we had received it was written: "You must cling to the terrain tooth and nail." That sentence, with its literary air, was a rather good rendering of the position in which we all found ourselves. The trenches were improvised—on naked ground, with no deep digging, no bags of dirt, no parapets. More than trenches, what we'd found were individual foxholes, scattered here and there, which each of us had tried to deepen, if not exactly with our teeth, then surely in large part with our nails. We were stretched out on our bellies, our heads just barely protected behind a rock or some clump of earth. Instinctively, with every burst of machine-gun fire, every hissing of a grenade, we made an even greater effort to squeeze our bodies into a smaller space and to become less vulnerable, pressing ourselves even further into the ground, flattened against the surface of the soil.

Aside from all the pieces of field artillery set up in the Asiago basin, the artillery bombardment was carried out by big-caliber guns. For the first time, the 305mms and 420mms went into action on the high plateau. These last none of us had even seen yet. The trajectory made a special noise, a gigantic rumbling, which was interrupted from time to time, only to come back in an even louder crescendo, right up to the final explosion. Tornadoes of earth, rock, and body fragments flew up into the air, way high up, and fell back down far away. The hole produced by the explosion was big enough for an entire platoon. I thought about the major's armor. Explosions rarely hit the front line. Most of the shells hit behind us, toward the two big lateral ravines around Mount Spill. The whole terrain was shaking under our feet. An earthquake was devastating the mountain. Even now, at such a great distance in time, when our self-esteem, as part of an involuntary psychological process, highlights only those past feelings that seem most noble while repressing the others, I can still remember the dominant idea of those initial minutes. More than an idea, an agitation, an instinctive impulse: Save yourself.

Cadet Perini stood straight up in the middle of his men and took off. Having suddenly popped up, almost as though a grenade had dug him out of the bowels of the earth, he turned his back on his platoon and bolted to the rear. Very young, and sickly, he had never taken part in combat. The major saw the cadet before I did, when he passed by us, and he pointed the boy out to me. Without a helmet, his face contorted, he was screaming, "Hurrah! Hurrah!" It's likely that, in the throes of panic, the Austrians had penetrated so deeply inside him that he was cheering for them.

"Shoot that coward!" the major shouted at me.

I heard the major but I just looked at the cadet without moving. The major didn't move either. He kept on shouting at me, "Shoot that coward!"

The cadet had already gone several hundred meters and disappeared behind a mound, flying, but the major, like a broken record repeating the same phrase ad infinitum, continued to shout monotonously, "Shoot that coward! Shoot that coward!

To persuade him to change the subject of conversation, I took the canteen of brandy from his orderly, who was standing beside me, and offered it to him. He grasped it in his hands avidly, as though all he'd been doing until then was asking me for a drink. He wiped the wet soil from his lips with the back of his hand and took a long drink.

We were all parched with thirst. All along the line, at every instant, you could see someone throw back their shoulders, unlatch their canteen, and drink. A few minutes of shelling were sufficient to make our mouths, tongues, and throats bone dry, to make us desire, madly, a drop of anything that would quench our thirst and abate our frantic anxiety. The little brandy we had been issued in Foza was already gone. In the midst of that whirlwind of grenades, the soldiers got up, one after another, ran over to the crevasse, picked up a fistful of snow, and ran back to their posts. Those furious races back and forth were the only actions that animated that otherwise motionless scene and gave us the certainty that there were still some survivors on the line. In my pockets I had some leaves that I had picked up on Mount Spill, and I chewed on them. Everyone was smoking. When the major finished one cigarette, he immediately lit another, chain-smoking the whole time.

The grenades were exploding so close to our group that I couldn't hear what the major was saying to me anymore.

He took out a piece of paper, penciled a few words on it, and handed it to me. The note said: "Get on your feet and tell me what's happening." I stood up and looked. The battalion, immobile, looked like a long line of bushes. To our right, at the center of his company, Lieutenant Grisoni was standing straight, his hands in his pockets and his pipe in his mouth. I didn't notice anything else on the line.

The shelling continued, but the battalion held out.

How long the shelling lasted I couldn't say. I couldn't have said even at the time. During a battle you lose all sense of time. You think it's ten in the morning and it's five in the afternoon.

Suddenly, one of our machine guns opened fire. I stood up to look. The Austrians were attacking.

VI

I believe everyone who experienced the events of that day will see them again on their deathbeds.

While our machine gun fired away, the shelling stopped. The enemy had attacked at the very moment when the artillery had stopped firing.

The Austrians were attacking en masse, in closed order, their battalions aligned side by side. Their rifles hanging from their shoulder straps, they weren't shooting. Convinced that, after that bombardment, there wasn't a living soul left in our lines, they were advancing blithely. They came forward, singing an anthem of war, of which all that reached our ears was the echo of the incomprehensible chorus.

"Hurrah!"

And the chorus started up again.

Our lines were agitated by a confused moving about. The officers and warrant officers were hunched over, running back and forth to check their units. The shelling had hit them only partially. The major was shouting, "Attention! Open fire! Ready to counterattack! Bayonets on!"

The officers repeated the order and there was a convulsive

clamor of voices. Our battalion was coming back to life. The front line opened fire. Of our two machine guns, only one was firing. The other had been wiped out in the shelling. We couldn't see any enemy columns except the ones in front of us, but the attack must have been simultaneous, off to our right as well.

The enemy battalions were advancing in step, slowly, impeded by rocks and underbrush. Our machine gun was firing away rabidly, without pause. It was manned by the commander of the machine-gun section, Lieutenant Ottolenghi. We saw entire units fall to the ground, mowed down. Their comrades shifted to the left or right to keep from stepping on the fallen. The battalions got back into formation. They struck up their chorus again. The tide was rolling in.

"Hurrah!"

The wind was blowing against us. From the Austrian ranks came an odor of brandy, thick, condensed, as though it were bursting forth from some dank wine cellars, closed for years. During the singing and the shouts of "Hurrah!" it seemed as though the cellars were throwing open their doors and inundating us with brandy. That brandy flowed into my nostrils in waves, filtered down to my lungs, and stayed down there in an odorous blend of tar, gasoline, resin, and sour wine.

"Ready for the counterattack!" the major kept on shouting, on his feet, in the middle of the soldiers.

My attention was mainly directed at the captain of the 11th. He was already on his feet, standing straight, bareheaded, his face smeared with mud. He was holding a pistol in his right hand and his helmet in his left. He was just a few meters from us.

"Cowards!" he shouted. "Come right ahead, if you've got the courage! Come on! Come on!"

And he looked back and forth, first to the far-off Austrians, who were advancing, and then to his own men, who were still on the ground looking up at him in amazement. It was his helmet that, his arm sticking straight out, he was pointing at them like a pistol. And it was his pistol that, mistaking it for a helmet, he was trying to put on his head. The more his efforts turned out to be in vain, the more he became exasperated and screamed. He beat himself on the head violently with the pistol, and blood was streaming down his face. The captain looked like a bloody fury.

"Hurrah!

By now the Austrians were no more than fifty meters away.

"Bayonets!" the major yelled.

"Savoy!" the units yelled, throwing themselves forward.

I've never had a very clear idea of what happened in that battle. The brandy fumes had left me bewildered. But I saw distinctly that, in front of us, to our left, a group of three men with a machine gun who had detached from the Austrian formation and deployed behind a rock. The tac-tac-tac of the Schwarzlose machine gun followed their rapid movement. A swath of bullets whistled all around us. The major was beside me. His pistol fell from his hand; he raised his arms up high and fell backward, on top of me. I tried to hold him up but I fell to the ground, too. His orderly threw himself down beside him to lift him up. The major just lay there, motionless. The orderly unbuttoned his battle jacket, and we saw his chest covered with blood. His metal armor, layered like fish scales, was full of holes.

I got up and charged forward again. The clash between us and the Austrians had already been joined. Chaotically mixed together, the two sides came to a halt. The Austrian units pulled back, in step, rifles hanging from their shoulder straps, just as they had advanced. The unexpected resistance had thrown them into confusion. Our men, held back by their officers, bellies to the ground, opened fire on the Austrians' backs. I saw just a few of them fall. Their units, shoulder to shoulder, quickly disappeared behind the mounds. The wind kept on blowing, inundating us with brandy fumes.

The poor major had given clear orders for the counterattack. Once the Austrians had been driven back, he wanted our battalion to reoccupy the positions it held at the start. I saw to it that his orders were executed swiftly. The most senior officer in the battalion, Captain Canevacci, took over command of the battalion.

The terrain was strewn with dead bodies, but we had held out. We were all out of stretchers so we carried back the wounded as best we could. Lieutenant Grisoni, carried by his arms by two soldiers, his leg broken, pipe in mouth, came off the mountain whistling.

We got the units back in order and called the roll.

Hours went by. The sun was bending down toward Mount Pasubio and we were still on the line, without any news. The only signs of life from the Austrians were some volleys from their field artillery. The calm after the storm.

A written order from the sector commander got us back on the move. The order read as follows: "The enemy has been able to take and hold positions in several points. The Mount Fior line is no longer sustainable. Upon receiving this order the battalion shall make an orderly retreat to Mount Spill."

"Retreat to Mount Spill?" shouted Captain Canevacci, inveighing against the dispatch carrier. "And tomorrow another order will tell us to attack Mount Fior and that will be the end of us."

The captain could not abide abandoning such an important position to the enemy without further resistance.

"I'll get myself shot," he said over and over again, "but I am not going to retreat."

The dispatch carrier asked for a written receipt of the order he had delivered, but the captain refused.

"Tell them I will not give the order to retreat.... Tell them they can shoot me for refusal to obey, but that this battalion, as long as I'm in command, will not abandon Mount Fior."

I tried to make him see that the sector commander was the only one competent to decide about the situation and that we had none of the elements necessary to determine that he was wrong. That, in any case, we had to obey. The captain would not be convinced and sent the dispatch carrier back without a written receipt. He was a career officer and he was taking an enormous risk. Even after the dispatch carrier left I tried, to no avail, to get him to reconsider his decision. He was convinced that the abandonment of the mountain was tantamount to treason. Not even half an hour later a corporal from our regiment command arrived with another written order. The colonel had signed it personally. If the battalion, the order began, does not begin the ordered retreat, Captain Canevacci should consider himself relieved of his command.

"I'm relieved of my command? But the Italian army is under the command of the Austrians! It's a disgrace!"

He was furious. But when his fury passed, he made up his mind to obey. We retreated by companies and we carried our wounded back with us. When the last company withdrew from Mount Fior, the rest of our battalion, deployed between two other battalions, was already in position on Mount Spill.

We'd left behind some rearguard lookouts. They were to keep firing a few rifle shots every so often and retreat at the first sign of an enemy advance. The Austrians didn't notice we'd retreated until the late afternoon. In the end, they had some doubts and sent out a line of patrols. Our lookouts fired their last shots and came back to rejoin the battalion. The enemy patrols found Mount Fior deserted.

I was on the line on the highest point of Mount Spill, looking over at Mount Fior. The Austrians came pouring onto the mountain in a disorderly stream. In less than half an hour the line we had abandoned was occupied by a group of their battalions. The entire crest of the mountain was teeming with troops.

I believe it was about six or seven o'clock in the evening. I noticed an unusual ferment among the enemy positions. What was going on? The battalions were moving around, yelling, saluting. The entire mass of them, like a single man, stood up and an acclamation came down to us from the mountaintop.

"Hurrah!"

I couldn't understand their celebration. It was something more than the joy of having taken a position without resistance. Why all that enthusiasm?

I turned around to look back and I understood.

Behind us, incandescent under the day's last rays of sunshine, like an immense blanket dotted with glistening pearls, the plains of the Veneto stretched out as far as the eye could see. Beneath us, Bassano and the River Brenta; and then, farther off and to the right, Verona, Vicenza, Treviso, Padova. All the way back, to the left, Venice. Venice!

VII

The lieutenant general in command of the division, held to be responsible for the unjustified abandonment of Mount Fior, was given the ax. In his stead, the division command was taken over by Lieutenant General Leone. The daily order issued by the commandant of the Third Army presented him to us as "a soldier of proven tenacity and time-tested bravery." I met him for the first time on Mount Spill, near the battalion command. His orderly officer told me he was the new division commander and I introduced myself.

Standing at attention, I gave him the rundown on the battalion.

"At ease," the general told me in a decorous and authoritative tone. "Where have you been until now in this war?"

"Always with this brigade, on the Carso."

"Have you ever been wounded?"

"No, sir, general."

"What, you've been on the front line for the entire war and you've never been wounded? Never?"

"Never, general. Unless we want to consider a few flesh

wounds that I've had treated here in the battalion, without going to the hospital."

"No, no, I'm talking about serious wounds, grave wounds."

"Never, general."

"That's very odd. How do you explain that?"

"The exact reason escapes me, general, but I'm certain that I've never been gravely wounded."

"Have you taken part in all the combat operations of your brigade?"

"All of them."

"The 'black cats'?"

"The 'black cats.'"

"The 'red cats'?"

"And the 'red cats,' general."

"Very odd indeed. Are you perhaps timorous?"

I thought: To put a guy like this in his place it would take at least a general in command of an army corps. Since I didn't answer right away, the general, still somber, repeated the question.

"I believe not," I replied.

"You believe or are you sure?"

"In war, you can never be sure of anything," I replied politely, and added with the hint of a smile that was intended to be conciliatory, "not even that you're sure."

The general didn't smile. No, I think smiling was almost impossible for him. He was wearing a steel helmet with the neck strap fastened, which gave his face a metallic look. His mouth was invisible, and if he hadn't had a mustache you would have said he had no lips. His eyes were gray and hard, always open, like the eyes of a nocturnal bird of prey.

The general changed the subject.

"Do you love war?"

I hesitated. Should I answer this question or not? There were officers and soldiers within earshot. I decided to respond.

"I was in favor of the war, general, and at my university I was a representative of the interventionists."

"That," said the general in a tone that was chillingly calm, "pertains to the past. I'm asking you about the present."

"War is a serious thing, too serious, and it's hard to say . . . it's hard . . . Anyway, I do my duty." And since he was staring at me dissatisfied, I added, "All of my duty."

"I didn't ask you," the general said, "if you do or do not do your duty. In war, everyone has to do his duty, because if you don't, you risk being shot. You understand me. I asked you if you love or don't love war."

"Love war!" I exclaimed, a bit discouraged.

The general stared at me, inexorable. His eyes had grown larger. It looked to me like they were spinning in their sockets.

"Can't you answer?" the general insisted.

"Well, I believe . . . certainly . . . I think I can say . . . that I have to believe . . ."

I was looking for a possible answer.

"Just what is it that you believe, then?"

"I believe, personally, I mean to say just for myself, generally speaking, I couldn't really affirm that I have a special predilection for war."

"Stand at attention!"

I was already standing at attention.

"Ah, so you're for peace, are you?" Now the general's voice was tinged with surprise and disdain. "For peace! Just like some meek little housewife, consecrated to hearth and home, to her kitchen, her bedroom, her flowers, to her flowers, to her sweet little flowers! Is that how it is, lieutenant?"

"No, general."

"And what kind of peace is it that you desire?"

"A peace . . ." And inspiration came to my aid. "A victorious peace."

The general seemed reassured. He asked me a few more routine questions and then asked me to accompany him on a tour of the front line.

When we were in the trench, at the highest and closest point to the enemy lines, facing Mount Fior, he asked me, "How far is it here, between our trenches and the Austrians'?"

"About two hundred fifty meters," I replied.

The general took a long look and said, "Here, it's two hundred thirty meters."

"Probably."

"Not probably. Certainly."

We had made a solid trench, with rocks and big clods of earth. The men could walk up and down its entire length without being seen. The lookouts observed and shot through loopholes, under cover. The general looked out from the loophole, but he wasn't satisfied. He had a pile of rocks made at the foot of the parapet and climbed upon them, his eyes behind binoculars. Standing straight up, he was uncovered from his chest to his head.

"General," I said, "the Austrians have some excellent snipers and it's dangerous to expose yourself like that."

The general didn't answer me. Standing straight, he kept on looking through his binoculars. Two rifle shots rang out from the enemy line. The bullets whistled past the general. He remained impassive. Two more shots followed the first two, and one of them grazed the trench. Only then, composed and unhurried, did he come down. I looked at him up close. His face displayed arrogant indifference, but his eyes were spinning. They looked like the wheels of a race car.

The lookout who was on duty just a few steps away from him continued looking out of his loophole. But, attracted by the exceptional show, some soldiers and a corporal from the 12th Company, then on the line, had stopped in the trench, all huddled together next to the general, and they were looking at him, more distrustful than impressed. They no doubt found in the division commander's overly audacious attitude some very good reasons to ponder, with a certain amount of apprehension, their own fate. The general gazed at his onlookers with satisfaction.

"If you're not afraid," he said, turning to the corporal, "do what your general just did."

"Yes, sir," the corporal replied. And leaning his rifle against the trench wall, he climbed up on the pile of rocks.

Instinctively, I grabbed the corporal by the arm and made him come down.

"The Austrians have been alerted now," I said, "and they certainly won't miss on the next shot."

With a chilling glance, the general reminded me of the difference in rank that separated me from him. I let go of the corporal's arm and didn't say another word.

"But there's nothing to it," said the corporal, and he climbed back up on the pile.

As soon as he looked out he was greeted by a barrage of rifle fire. The Austrians, roused by his previous apparition, were waiting with their guns pointed. The corporal remained unhurt. Impassive, his arms leaning on the parapet, his chest exposed to enemy fire, he kept his eyes to the front.

"Bravo!" the general cried. "You can get down now."

A single shot came from the enemy trench. The corporal fell backward and landed on top of us. I bent over him. The bullet had hit him in the top of the chest, under his collarbone, going in one side and out the other. Blood was coming out of his mouth. His eyes slits, gasping for breath, he murmured, "It's nothing, lieutenant."

The general bent over him, too. The soldiers looked at him, hate in their eyes.

"He's a hero," the general commented. "A real hero."

When he straightened up, his eyes again met mine. Just for a second. In that instant, I recalled having seen those very same eyes, cold and rotating, in the mental hospital of my hometown during a visit we'd made there with our professor of forensic medicine.

He looked for his change purse and pulled out a silver one-lira coin.

"Here," he said to the corporal. "You can drink a glass of wine the first chance you get."

The wounded man shook his head in refusal and hid his hands. The general stood there with the lira in his fingers and, after a moment's hesitation, let it drop onto the corporal. Nobody picked it up.

The general continued his inspection of the line and when he got to the end of my battalion, he dispensed me from following him.

I made my way back to the battalion command. The whole line was in an uproar. The news of what had happened had already made it around the entire sector. For their part, the stretcher-bearers who had carried the corporal to the first-aid post had recounted the episode to everyone they ran into. Captain Canevacci was beside himself.

"The people in command of the Italian army are Austrians!" he exclaimed. "Austrians in front of us, Austrians at our backs, Austrians in our midst!"

Near the battalion command I ran into Lieutenant Colonel Abbati again. That was the name of the officer from the 301st Infantry. He was supposed to go up to the front line with his battalion. He knew about the incident too. I called out to him. He didn't answer. When he got up close to me, he said, worried, "The military art follows its course."

He stretched out his arm to unlatch the canteen I was

wearing on my belt. I rushed to offer it to him. Looking distracted, a vague look in his eyes, he took it delicately in hand. He held it up to his ear and shook it; it wasn't empty. He took out the cork and held it up to his lips to drink. But he stopped suddenly, with a look on his face of amazement and disgust, as though he'd seen the head of a snake spring forth from the mouth of the canteen.

"Coffee and water!" he exclaimed in a tone of compassion. "Look, kid, start drinking. Otherwise you'll end up in the loony bin, too, like your general."

VIII

A man as bold as General Leone couldn't remain idle. We still didn't have a single piece of artillery on the high plateau. All the same he ordered an attack on Mount Fior for the day of the sixteenth. My battalion stayed behind, as brigade reserve, and I didn't take part in the operation.

We had a few days of relaxation. The enemy artillery remained inactive. We suffered no casualties, not even one man wounded. All those hours spent out in the sun, lying on the rocks, our eyes wandering, along with our dreams, over the plains of the Veneto! Life was so far away from us!

The division commander knew no rest. He wanted to take Mount Fior at all costs. Every day he was on the front line measuring distances, making drawings, devising plans. In the end he had come up with a plan for a sneak attack, with bayonets, in broad daylight, which my battalion, the one with the most experience on top of the mountain, was supposed to execute.

The attack was set for the twenty-sixth; the Austrians withdrew on the twenty-fourth. Our resistance on Mount Pasubio and the great offensive unleashed by the Russians in

Galicia had forced them to suspend their operations on the high plateau. They abandoned Mount Fior, just as we had. And we took it back the same way they had taken it from us. Their retreat, which probably lasted several days, was ably disguised. They left nothing on the front lines except some small and infrequent patrols. When we realized what was happening, we began our advance, and our only contact was some small skirmishes between patrols.

The general, intrepid in the war of position, was even more so in the war of maneuver. He ordered that our troops must never, neither day nor night, lose contact with the enemy's rear guard, and he compelled the general in command of the brigade to take part personally in the movements of our advance guard. Despite his advanced age, the brigade commander put himself at the head of the first company of our advance guard and was killed in a skirmish between patrols. It was a huge loss for the entire brigade; the soldiers loved him.

When the division commander learned of his death, his ardor doubled.

"We must avenge him!" he said to all the units. "We must avenge him as soon as possible!"

The general's burning desire for revenge was abated, though not totally extinguished, by the reaction of the enemy's rear guard. Their patrols, armed with machine guns, fought with unrelenting tenacity, and they willingly sacrificed themselves to block our advance. A lot of machine guns fell into our hands that way, defended to the death by their users. But other patrols, further back, in a dominant position on high ground, repeatedly forced us to deploy in combat formation and lose a lot of time. The general lost his usual calm. He climbed a fir tree and installed himself on the top, like the commander of a ship with a command post on the maintop, and shouted, "Forward, brave soldiers, forward! Forward to avenge your brigade commander!"

"If we really wanted to avenge our brigade commander we'd have two dead generals today," Captain Canevacci said to me. "And our revenge would create a vacancy in the division commander's post."

He was beginning to find the general unbearable.

Even if our soldiers had been endowed with ferocious determination, it would have been mitigated by the hilarity provoked by the general's urgings, shouted from such an extraordinary position.

"If the general stays up in the tree and builds a nest there, the division will be saved," Captain Canevacci remarked, his eyebrow raised. "If he comes down, the division is lost."

Our battalion had brought with it the advance guard battalion, which was supposed to spread out to avoid offering an easy target to the enemy machine guns and be prepared for a possible counteroffensive. Our advance was proceeding slowly; it was hard to make much progress under fire and in the woods, where the footpaths and cattle trails were not always practicable. The companies had to keep covered behind shrubs and never lose contact with each other.

As evening was coming on, the enemy resistance became less active. Their patrols kept up the shooting, but if they were going to retreat they couldn't wait around to make a stand against our bayonets. We accelerated our pursuit and avoided casualties except for a few wounded. The general came down from the tree and marched between the 2nd Battalion and ours, on foot, followed by his mule and a muleteer holding the reins.

A voice shouted from up ahead, "Halt! Backpacks on the ground."

"Who was it that yelled?" the general asked, glowering.

It was a liaison trooper in the 7th Company, 2nd Battalion. When he reached the intersection between two trails, he advised the units behind him to stop. The scouts needed time to figure out the direction of the trails and communicate which of the two was the one to follow. One of them had just been shot dead and the others couldn't risk moving ahead until the terrain had been reconnoitered. The soldier who shouted was only doing what he'd been ordered to do. Captain Zavattari, in command of the 6th Company, reported to the general.

"Have that man shot," the general ordered.

Have that man shot! Captain Zavattari was a reserve officer. In civilian life he was a division chief at the Ministry of Public Instruction. He was the oldest captain in the regiment. The order to have a soldier shot was an inconceivable absurdity. Measuring his words, he found the way to put it to the general.

"Have him shot this very instant," the general replied without a moment's hesitation.

The captain left and came back to the general a few minutes later. He had gone to the intersection of the trails and personally interrogated the liaison trooper.

"Did you have him shot?" the general asked him.

"No, sir. The soldier didn't do anything he wasn't ordered to do. He never thought that by shouting 'Halt! Backpacks on the ground,' he was emitting a shout of fatigue or indiscipline. He was only trying to transmit an order to his comrades. The scouts had just had one of their men killed. The halt was necessary to give them time to reconnoiter the terrain."

"Have him shot anyway," the general replied coldly. "We need to make an example of him!"

"But how can I have a soldier shot without any kind of proceeding and when he hasn't committed a crime?"

The general didn't share his juridical mindset. Those legalistic arguments irritated him.

"Have him shot immediately," he shouted, "and don't force me to have my military police intervene against you as well."

The general was assisted by two military policemen in service to the division command. The captain understood that, in those circumstances, all he could do was find some ploy to save the soldier, whose life was hanging by a thread.

"Yes, sir," the captain responded firmly.

"Execute the order and report back to me at once."

The captain went back up to the head of his company, which had stopped the advance and was waiting for orders. He had a squad fire a salvo of rifle shots against a tree trunk and ordered the stretcher-bearers to put the body of the dead scout on a stretcher. The operation completed, he returned to the general, followed by the stretcher. The other soldiers knew nothing of his macabre stratagem and they all looked at each other aghast.

"The soldier's been shot," the captain said.

The general saw the stretcher, stiffened to attention, and saluted proudly. He was moved.

"Salute the martyrs of the fatherland! In war, discipline is painful but necessary. Let us honor our dead!"

The stretcher passed through the crestfallen soldiers.

At dusk we ceased our pursuit. The advance-guard battalion stopped and implemented security measures for the night. My battalion stayed back, on this side of the Val di Nos, on the edge of the woods, opposite Croce Sant'Antonio. A sudden hailstorm had made the night freezing cold. We were all drenched. We each had a blanket and a canvas tarp but we were still in our summer uniforms, no wool, just as we had left the Carso. The cold in the bivouac was unbearable. Around midnight we were given permission to light fires. Distance and the woods protected us from being seen by the enemy.

We were gathered around the bonfires, the fir trees burning with the pungent smell of resin. Whispering, the men commented on the events of the day.

Then a stentorian shout resounded in the wood. "Stay alert! Stay alert! Woe to those who sleep! The enemy is near! Stay alert!

Who was it?

"Stay alert! A sleeping soldier is a dead soldier. Stay alert! Your general isn't sleeping! Stay alert!"

It was General Leone.

In the silence of the night, his voice was cavernous. I got up and left the battalion commander sitting on a rock by the fire. I stopped in the middle of several groups of soldiers from the 12th Company. The men, huddled around the fires, didn't notice my presence. I moved in closer to one of the squads so the warmth of the flames would reach me, too, and I looked in the direction the voice was coming from.

"Stay alert! Your general is coming through, your general isn't sleeping. Stay alert!"

Slowly, the voice came closer. The general was walking in the middle of our battalion.

"That nut doesn't sleep," whispered a soldier from the 12th.

"Better a dead general than a sleepless general," another remarked.

"Stay alert! Your general is coming through!"

"Now he's coming right at us," another soldier said.

"Isn't anybody going to take a shot at that butcher?" murmured the same man who had spoken first.

"Sure, I'll fire one at him. I'll fire one at him with pleasure," said an old soldier who hadn't spoken yet and had seemed intent only on getting warm, beside the sergeant.

The men of the squad were so close together, one right next to the other, around the fire, that the firelight lit up all their faces and I could clearly recognize all of them. The sergeant was on one knee, his arms crossed over his chest and his hands open near his head to protect his face from the heat of the flames. He didn't move or say a word.

"If he shows his face, I'll shoot him," the old soldier continued. I saw him grab his rifle, open the breechblock, and check the magazine.

"Stay alert! Stay alert!" the general shouted.

He came into view, between two fires, about fifty meters away. Under his helmet he had a scarf wrapped around his neck that fell down onto his shoulders. A big, gray cape went all the way down to his ankles and covered his whole body. He was walking awkwardly, his hands around his mouth like a megaphone. Barely illuminated by the firelight, he looked like a ghost.

"Stay alert!"

The old soldier slowly raised his rifle to take aim.

"Hey," I said, "the general doesn't want to sleep."

The soldier lowered his rifle. The sergeant jumped to his feet and offered me his place by the fire.

IX

We continued our pursuit the next day. After moving past Croce Sant'Antonio, the advance-guard battalion proceeded through the forest toward the grassy basin of Casara Zebio and Mount Zebio. As it advanced, it appeared more and more probable that the largest part of the enemy force had stopped in the highlands. Their resistance had become tenacious again. It was clear that the last Austrian units, in contact with our patrols, were supported by troops nearby. Given the slowness of our progress, my battalion, once we'd crossed the Val di Nos, remained inactive the whole day, waiting to be called into action.

The advance-guard 2nd Battalion received orders to stop and dig in. During the night, our battalion replaced it. When we arrived, one trench line had already been dug, hurriedly, on the outer edge of the woods. There were still some fir trees in front of us, but few and far between, as they always are on the edges of high-altitude fir woods. The terrain was still covered with bushes. Further away and higher up, several hundred meters ahead, some rocky mountain peaks loomed among the tops of the last fir trees. We could probably expect the stiffest resistance at their feet.

At dawn, Captain Canevacci and I were on the line with the 9th Company. We were waiting for the arrival of the machine-gun unit, which had stayed behind. The captain in command of the 9th was keeping watch over the terrain in front of the line with a group of sharpshooters. We were next to him, lying on the ground, behind a mound. Canevacci was looking through his binoculars.

Among the bushes, less than a hundred meters away, an enemy patrol came into view. There were seven of them, walking in single file. Convinced they were nowhere near our line, out of sight, they were proceeding parallel to our trench, walking straight up, rifles in hand, packs on their backs. They were exposed from their knees up. The captain of the 9th gestured to the sharpshooters, gave the order to fire, and the patrol crumbled to the ground.

"Bravo!" exclaimed Captain Canevacci.

One of our squads moved out of the trench on all fours. Behind them the entire line had their rifles pointed. The squad disappeared, slithering on their bellies, into the bushes.

We were expecting the squad to come back in carrying the fallen, but time was going by. Our men had to advance very cautiously to avoid an ambush. Captain Canevacci was losing patience. The machine-gun unit still hadn't arrived. What if they'd gotten lost in the forest, in the middle of the other units? To keep from losing more time I went back to look for them.

I found them half a kilometer farther back, in contact with

the units of the 2nd Battalion. When I saw them, a dramatic scene was being played out, General Leone, alone on his mule, was climbing up a rocky slope between the 2nd Battalion and the machine-gun unit. As the mule was moving along the edge of a steep drop, about sixty-five feet, it stumbled and the general fell to the ground. The mule, unperturbed, kept walking along the edge of the cliff. The general was still hanging on to the reins, with half of his body dangling over the precipice. With each step, the mule yanked its head from side to side, trying to shake him off. At any moment the general might fall off the cliff. There were a lot of soldiers nearby who saw him, but nobody made a move. I could see them all very clearly; some of them winked at each other, smiling.

Any minute now the mule would free itself of the general. A soldier rushed out from the ranks of the machine-gun unit and threw himself down on the ground in time to save him. Without losing his composure, as though he had trained especially for accidents of this kind, the general remounted his mule, continued on his way, and disappeared. The soldier, back on his feet, looked around, satisfied. He had saved the general.

When his comrades from the machine-gun unit reached him, I witnessed a savage assault. They mauled him furiously, pummeling him with punches. The soldier fell to the ground on his back. His comrades jumped on top of him.

"Son of a bitch! You miserable bastard!"

"Leave me alone! Help!"

Punches and kicks slammed into the poor wretch, who was powerless to defend himself.

"Here! Take that! Who paid you to be the imbecile?"

"Help!"

"Save the general! Admit that you were paid by the Austrians!"

"Leave me alone! I didn't do it on purpose. I swear I didn't do it on purpose."

The commander of the machine-gun unit was nowhere to be seen. The beating had gone on too long. Since nobody, neither officers nor NCOs, intervened to stop it, I ran over to them.

"What's going on?" I shouted in a loud voice.

My presence surprised everyone. The aggressors dispersed. Only a couple of them remained where they were and stood at attention. I went over to the victim, held out my hand, and helped him up. By the time he was back on his feet, those few who had stayed had disappeared. I was standing there alone with the soldier. He had a black eye and a cheek covered with blood. He'd lost his helmet.

"What happened?" I asked him. "Why did they come after you like that?"

"It's nothing, lieutenant," he muttered under his breath.

And he turned his frightened gaze right and left, looking for his helmet, but also out of fear of being heard by his comrades.

"What do you mean, it's nothing? What about the black eye? And the blood on your face? You're half dead and it's nothing?"

Standing at attention, embarrassed, the soldier didn't respond. I insisted, but he didn't say another word.

We were both relieved of our embarrassment by the arrival of the commander of the machine gunners, Lieutenant Ottolenghi, the one who in the battle on Mount Fior, with just one gun still working, had saved the day. We were the same rank, but I was more senior. Without saying even a word to me, he went up to the soldier and yelled at him, "You imbecile! Today you dishonored our unit."

But what was I supposed to do, lieutenant?"

"What were you supposed to do? You should have done what everybody else did. Nothing. You should have done nothing. And even that was too much. A dumbass like you I don't even want him in my unit. I'm going to have you thrown out."

The soldier had found his helmet and was putting it back on his head.

"What were you supposed to do?" the lieutenant said again, with disdain. "You wanted to do something? Well then, you should have taken your bayonet and cut the reins and made the general fall off the cliff."

"What?" the soldier muttered. "I should have let the general die?"

"Yes, you cretin, you should have let him die. And if he wasn't going to die, then—since you wanted to do something no matter what the cost—you should have helped him die. Go back to the unit, and if the rest of them kill you, you'll have got what you deserve."

"Look," I said to him after the soldier had gone, "you'd better take things a little more seriously. In a few hours the whole brigade will know what happened."

"Whether they know or don't know makes no difference to me. On the contrary, it's better if they do know. That way, somebody might just get the idea to take a shot at that vampire."

He went on talking, still indignant. He stuck his hand in his pocket, pulled out a coin, tossed it into the air, and said to me, "Heads or tails?"

I didn't answer.

"Heads!" he shouted.

It was tails.

"You're lucky," he went on. "Tails. If it had been heads . . . if it had been heads . . ."

"What?" I asked.

"If it had been heads. . . . Well! Let's leave it for the next time."

As the machine-gun unit was joining the battalion, the squad from 9th Company was coming back to the trench, dragging the bodies of the fallen patrol. Six were dead, one was still alive. Their corporal was one of the dead. From their papers we determined they were Bosnians. The two captains were satisfied. Especially Canevacci, who was hoping they could obtain some useful information by interrogating the survivor. He had him taken to the first-aid station and immediately informed the division command, where an interpreter was on staff.

The six dead men were lying on the ground, one next to the other. We contemplated them, deep in thought. Sooner or later, for us, too, the time would come. But Captain Canevacci was too pleased. He stopped next to the body of the corporal and said to him, "Hey! My friend, if you had learned how to command a patrol you wouldn't be here right now. When you're out on patrol, the commander, first of all, has to see . . ."

He was interrupted by the captain of the 9th. With a finger on his mouth and a thin thread of a voice, he invited him to keep quiet. In front of us, from the same direction in which the patrol had fallen, but closer, there was a sound, like the buzzing of people having an argument. The captain looked to the front. The sharpshooters aimed their rifles. The battalion commander and I also kept quiet and made our way silently up to the line to have a look.

The sound was coming from the trunk of a big fir tree, illuminated in patches by the sunlight shining through the treetops. Two squirrels were jumping along the trunk, a few meters off the ground. Quick and nimble, they chased each other, hid, chased each other again, and hid again. Short little shrieks, like uncontainable laughter, marked their encounters each time they launched themselves with little hops from opposite sides of the trunk, the one against the other. And every time they stopped themselves in a circle of sunlight on the trunk, they stood straight up on their hind legs and, using their paws like hands, appeared to be offering each other compliments, caresses, and congratulations. The sunlight shone brightly on their white bellies and the tufts of their tails, which stood straight up like two brushes.

One of the sharpshooters looked over at the captain of the 9th and muttered,

"Shall we shoot?"

"Are you crazy?" the captain answered in surprise. "They're so cute."

Captain Canevacci went back over to the line of dead bodies.

"The patrol commander must see and not be seen . . . ," he said, continuing his sermon to the Bosnian corporal.

X

The enemy's line of resistance was gradually beginning to take shape. During the day, our advance patrols were no longer met by enemy patrols. The incoming rifle fire was from a continuous line and seemed to indicate an already prepared trench. We had gotten glimpses in several spots of barbed-wire entanglements. We stopped pushing forward. Our brigade occupied our army's most advanced position.

The whole day went by without any action. General Leone was preparing a nighttime attack. Just before dusk, word came that we should be prepared. We called in our patrols and got ready to launch the attack. Casks and goatskins of brandy were brought in on mules and we rationed it out to the troops.

This nighttime attack had us all worried. It was supposed to be conducted along the entire front. Where were we going to end up? What kind of enemy units would we run into? Patrols, like the general said, or solidly defended trenches, as we were led to believe by the entanglements we'd sighted? The soldiers drank and waited, edgy. Captain Canevacci had already drunk his ration of brandy and had started on mine.

It was already ten o'clock and the faint starlight failed to penetrate the darkness of the forest. The attack order hadn't reached us yet. Evidently, the general wanted it to be a surprise, not just for the Austrians, but for us, too. The battalion commander had amassed our battalion into a column. His plan was for just one company to attack. The others were not to move unless the first company was able to get through. We all stood there motionless, not saying a word. Nothing broke the silence of the night except the occasional canteen bumping into a rock or rifle butts knocking against each other.

The general had dreamed up the idea that our buglers should sound the attack—consternation for the enemy, incitement for us. When the notes sounded, all the units in the front line launched the assault. But in the same instant, the Austrians, alerted by our bugles, responded with machine-gun and rifle fire. For several minutes the noise was deafening. Our bugles kept blowing, the enemy lines kept firing. In front of us, hundreds of rockets shot into the air, one after another without interruption, and lit up our waves of attackers. Our companies, greeted by bursts of gunfire, were mowed down, thrown back before they could even reach the enemy lines.

Disorder reigned, and transporting the wounded added to the confusion. The surprise and the assault had failed, but our bugles, under the command of the general, who had them by his side, kept on blowing. It seemed as though he had decided to take the enemy positions by trumpet blast.

It wasn't until several hours later, when calm had settled in to replace the clamor, that we learned that the general was satisfied. All he had wanted was for the enemy to give away his positions and display his forces. This same result could have been achieved by coordinated reconnaissance conducted by a few patrols, but the division commander disdained such miserably banal tactics.

So our pursuit had come to an end. The enemy had stopped and dug in. There could be no further doubt: By withdrawing from Mount Fior, the Austrians had shortened their lines by about twenty kilometers and averted the risk of encirclement. They had passed from offense to defense. We'd no longer be dealing with combat between patrols and advance and rear guards. A new phase was beginning, a phase of battles between masses of troops supported by artillery. This would take time. We might even be in for a little rest.

That's what we thought. But not the division commander. The nighttime assault had given him the inspiration for a full-scale attack the next day.

The following morning, the brigade's battalions moved left, under Casara Zebio. The brigade was supposed to attack with four battalions, leaving only two battalions in reserve. My battalion was to attack on the extreme right of our formation. The only weapons available to us for this operation were our rifles. We had already used up our scant supply of hand grenades on Mount Fior. We didn't have even one piece of artillery to support us. The operation promised to be a tough one, but our units were still solid. The mules kept us supplied with cartridges and brandy.

My battalion began the assault at five in the afternoon. As soon as we received the order, the battalion swarmed out of the trench with all of its units in a single wave. The minute we made our move we were spotted. The enemy had us in his sights right from the start.

My memory of those hours is confused. There must have been no more than a hundred meters or so between our starting point and the enemy lines. The bushes were low to the ground and the trees few, but there were lots of stones and rocks. The order was to keep moving forward no matter what. We ran across the short space in a single burst. Captain Canevacci was in the lead and he was one of the first to go down. A bullet had hit him in the chest. The commander of the 9th Company, the only captain left in the battalion, also went down. A machine gun had riddled his legs. But the attack went on impetuously. The enemy fire couldn't hit us all because we were running, and the rocks, low as they were, deflected most of the fire.

Behind us, the terrain was instantly strewn with dead and wounded, but regardless the battalion made it to the enemy positions. I had left Captain Canevacci behind and found myself in the middle of the 9th Company, next to Lieutenant Santini, who had taken over command of the company. In front of us, an unbroken line of entanglements and chevaux-de-frise blocked our access to the trenches. A meter or two beyond them, the masonry walls of the trenches, improvised but high, protected the Austrian units. Leaning against the entanglements, standing up, we opened fire, too. The machine guns that, during our sprint forward, had hammered our right flank, couldn't hit us anymore. They strafed all the terrain behind us, but the more we went ahead, the farther we got out of their range. They kept on shooting, but to no avail. In front of us, only a few meters away, just one machine gun was firing on our units. Santini ordered the soldiers around him to concentrate their fire on it and they silenced it. From our left, at a hundred meters or so, another machine gun was raking us right down the line. If it kept on shooting we would be wiped out. We couldn't defend ourselves from its line of fire and we couldn't even see where it was shooting from. We threw ourselves to the ground, each of us looking for cover while we kept firing at the trenches, aiming at the loopholes, trying to overpower the firing from the closest sharpshooters. The noise of combat, on our flanks as well as in front of us, made it impossible to determine if the units on either side of us had had any more luck than we'd had.

How long we were in that position I can't remember. In combat, you lose your sense of time, always. The entanglements kept us from moving forward, the machine guns from going back. We had to remain motionless, plastered to the ground, without ever ceasing fire on the enemy loopholes, to keep from being killed under the entanglements. We would have been able to hold out in that position for a long time, until nightfall, and then retreat under the protection of darkness, but the machine gun to our left kept spitting out its relentless raking fire and the most exposed of our soldiers were dying all down the line.

If we could send someone back to report our situation to the battalion engaged on our left, it could counterbattery the machine gun. I couldn't spot a single officer. Lieutenant

Santini was occupied with firing on the enemy trenches. So sliding on my belly between the rocks and the bushes, then running in spurts, I shifted over to the left. It took me a long time, in part because the battalion on our left flank was farther to the left than I thought. The crackling of the machine-gun and rifle fire didn't let up. The 1st Battalion was still engaged, but it was farther back and better protected than ours. Behind the fir trees, among the rocks, there was a nonstop coming and going of dispatch carriers and wounded. I immediately tried to locate the battalion command. A soldier pointed it out to me and I ran toward it. It was set up behind a rock that was several meters high. The ground around it was covered with wounded. Orders, cries, shouts rose up from every direction. The whole place had an air of confusion and terror. The major in command of the battalion was standing against the trunk of a fir tree. I knew him well because I had eaten at his mess many times. Red in the face, he was shaking his hands at someone I couldn't see. He looked really upset.

"Hurry up!" he shouted.

But nobody appeared.

As I moved closer, the major went on. "Hurry up! Hurry up or I'll kill you! Give me the brandy! The brandy!"

He wasn't shouting anymore. He was screaming at the top of his lungs, and in a tone of command, as though he weren't speaking to a single person but to an entire unit, to a battalion in closed ranks. He said "brandy" in the same voice he would have used to say, on horseback, "battalion in column!" or "double column!"

Finally, as I was approaching, a breathless soldier appeared on the scene with a bottle of brandy in hand, held high at the end of his outstretched arm, almost like a flag. I stopped two steps short of the major, stood at attention, and saluted. He was a holding a pistol in his right hand and a sheet of paper in his left. He threw the paper to the ground and went over to the soldier, still screaming, "Give it to me! Give it to me!"

He brandished the bottle and, with a lightning move, sealed it to his mouth. His head tilted back, motionless, he looked paralyzed, like he was dead on his feet. The only sign of life came from his throat, guzzling down the liquor with gulps that sounded like groans.

I waited for him to finish drinking. He detached himself from the bottle with difficulty, his body clenched in pain. He gave it back to the soldier, half empty, and didn't move. I went up to him again. Fast and furious, not giving him a chance to answer, I told him the reason for my visit. He was looking at me, but his thoughts were elsewhere and he wasn't listening to me. I spoke in vain. He still had his pistol in hand and, to show me he was paying attention, pointed it at me. I pushed the pistol away, afraid it might go off. He let it be moved away, but immediately pointed it in the same direction. I pushed it away a second time and he pointed it at me again. I grabbed his closed fist and took the pistol away. He let it be taken from him without saying a word. I took the bullet out of the chamber, removed the magazine, and returned the pistol to him. He took it back with the same indifference with which he'd given it up. Then he smiled at me, but it seemed to me that someone else was smiling inside him. I interpreted that smile as his attempt to make me think he'd been joking. Since he wasn't talking and I was losing time, I left, hoping to find his adjutant.

The adjutant was dead, the other officers were engaged with the battalion, and the soldiers at the command couldn't reach them and didn't know where they were. All around us, the hissing of the machine guns' constant raking reminded me of a hurricane. The treetops, sawed off by the bursts of gunfire, came crashing down to the ground with an ominous shrieking sound.

After running here and there searching futilely, I went back up to join my battalion and passed by the 1st Battalion command post. The major was standing there motionless, in the same spot where I'd left him, pistol in hand, and he was still smiling.

XI

During the night, in groups, the battalion returned to its initial position. We had lost all our officers. Only Lieutenant Santini and I made it back unscathed. Lieutenant Ottolenghi was still alive, too. He had received an order to stay back with the machine guns and hadn't gone out on the assault. The companies had been reduced to half their size. It took us all night to carry off the dead and wounded and when, after calling the roll, Santini and I had a chance to talk, we both had to make an effort to keep from throwing ourselves into each other's arms.

The war of position was starting up again. Our dreams of a quick victory in a war of maneuver were going up in smoke. We were going to have to start all over again, like before, on the Carso.

There followed a few days of calm. The units had to be replenished. Every day brought fresh complements of officers and soldiers. Slowly, we forgot our dead, and we veterans and the new arrivals began to fraternize.

Opposite the enemy trenches, at varying distances between fifty and three hundred meters, following the lay of the land and the edge of the forest, we set about building our own trenches. They were our homes, which the Austrians, now on the defensive, surely didn't think of attacking. But we had to be prudent every second. Facing us were units of sharpshooters who never missed a shot. They didn't shoot very often, but always at our heads, and with exploding bullets.

The days of calm were soon over. The battalion was recomposed in a hurry. Another operation was in the air. Every day ammunition and gelignite tubes arrived.[10] They were the same as the ones we'd used on the Carso, two meters long, built to open breaches in the entanglements. And wire-cutting pliers arrived, too. The wire cutters and the tubes had never done us any good, but they arrived just the same. And brandy arrived, lots of brandy, so we were on the verge of a new operation.

Our commanders had established that the next attack was to be preceded by the widespread use of gelignite tubes to be set off the night before under the enemy entanglements. My battalion was to go into action first, along with the 1st Battalion of the 400th, to open up the point of attack for our companion regiment from the brigade. The 1st Battalion had also suffered serious losses, but it had been reconstituted. The major was back in command. He sent Lieutenant Mastini to me so we could agree on the hour and the other details of our common mission of placing the gelignite tubes on the same line of attack.

Mastini and I had been students at the same university. Younger than me, he was in his second year when I was in my fourth. Friends, and veterans of the Carso, we'd also run into each other a lot on the Asiago plateau.

We had made an inspection tour along the line and we were taking a break behind my battalion's trench. I was stretched out on the ground; he was sitting on a rock in the shade. Our talk turned to his battalion commander. Mastini shared my view that the major drank too much. I recounted to him the scene I had witnessed.

"Our major isn't a bad officer," Mastini said. "A lot of the time he's brave and sometimes even smart. But if he doesn't have his brandy he's incapable of making a move during an operation."

"Do you remember Pareto?" I asked him. "How he drank! And what a brain! The professors were in awe, all of them. He had to have been the brightest student in the whole university! But if he didn't drink he couldn't pass an exam. A little like your major. No brandy, no combat."

The conversation meandered over and through our memories of university life, which felt so far away to us: a dream. He called to mind one of our parties, one that had gone down in the annals because the white wine was old and nasty and His Excellency the Rector had started singing bass while a first-year student embraced the wife of the Prefect.

"So do you drink a lot now, too?" I asked. "The word is that in your battalion you all drink like sponges."

His only answer, expressed in a gesture so quick it seemed that my question had suddenly reminded him of something he'd forgotten, was to uncork his canteen and take a few sips. It must have been really good brandy, because it left in its wake an unbearable odor of gunpowder.

Putting the cork back in the canteen, he said, "I adore Homer's *Odyssey* because every canto comes with a goatskin of wine."

"Wine," I said, "not brandy."

"Yeah," he observed, "it's curious. Really curious. Neither the *Odyssey* nor the *Iliad* has the slightest trace of liquor."

"Try to imagine it," I said, "Diomedes drinking down a bulging goatskin of brandy before going out on patrol."

We had one foot in Troy and one on the Asiago plateau. I can still see my good friend, with his smile of skeptical good-heartedness, pulling out of the inside pocket of his battle jacket a big stainless steel cigarette case, wartime heart protector, and offering me a cigarette. I accepted and lit his cigarette and mine. He kept on smiling, thinking of his answer.

"Anyway . . ."

And again, after inhaling a mouthful of smoke, "Anyway . . . If Hector had drunk a little brandy, some good brandy, Achilles might have had some trouble on his hands . . ."

For a brief second I too caught a glimpse of Hector pulling up short after his hurried and less than completely justified flight, under the gaze of his fellow citizens, spectators on the city walls, unlatching an elegant goatskin of cognac from his gold embroidered leather belt, Andromeda's gift, and drinking from it, in Achilles' face.

I've forgotten a lot of things about the war, but I'll never forget that moment. I was watching my friend smile between one mouthful of smoke and another. A single gunshot rang out from the enemy trench. He bowed his head, the cigarette still between his lips, and from a newly formed red spot on his forehead, a thin line of blood came streaming out. Slowly, he folded in on himself and fell on my feet. I lifted him up, dead.

That night we put the gelignite tubes in place. We had ten of them at the battalion command, piled on top of each other like logs. We were supposed to set off all ten. The young officers didn't know how to deploy them, so Lieutenant Santini and I directed the operation. Placing gelignite tubes to explode under the enemy entanglements, at night, on a well-covered terrain, was an extremely easy operation for anyone who was used to going out on patrol. Even if the enemy line started shooting, the danger was minimal. But you had to have a good set of nerves.

We chose our soldiers among volunteers from our battalion. The regiment command offered a reward of ten lire for each volunteer. You needed two men for each tube: ten tubes, twenty men. Nine went with Santini and nine with me. Uncle Francesco was one of the volunteers. I chose him to come with me.

I had a group of veterans from the Carso in my group and there was no need for lengthy explanations. At the appointed hour, having drunk our brandy, we climbed out of the trench, my group on the left, toward the 400th, Santini's on the right. We crawled out of the same opening and fanned out, in pairs, leaving about ten meters between one pair and the next. The enemy trenches were about sixty meters away.

If you're not used to it, leaving the shelter of the trench can make you feel a bit uneasy, suddenly finding yourself out in the open, facing the rifle shots of the enemy lookouts. A rookie says, "I've been spotted. The next shot is for me." But instead it's nothing. The lookouts shoot, straight ahead from their post, without a precise target, by chance, in the dark.

It was a dark night. We carried the tubes by hand. I was in front, Uncle Francesco in back. Where we felt safe we walked standing up; where we were more exposed, on all fours. The lookouts kept on firing, one shot and then another, without agitation. But where did all those bullets end up? We didn't hear even one come close to us.

A flare went up in front of us, then another to our right, and then still another.

"Maybe someone gave the alarm?" I thought. Holding our breath, standing up, just as we were when we'd been surprised by the first flare, we stood there motionless for several seconds, until the last flare fell to the ground and went out. The lookouts' shooting continued. At a slow pace, as before. They were routine flares. We hadn't been spotted.

We walked ahead slowly, stopping every few steps. The sound of our footsteps was covered by the noise of the lookouts' gunfire. Our lookouts kept on shooting, too, as they had before we left the trench, but into the air, to make noise without taking the risk of hitting us. But we still had to proceed with caution; an enemy patrol might be lying in wait behind the bushes we were forced to go by. More flares were set off, now to our left, now to our right. Standing still under the light of the flares, we blended in with the bushes and the tree trunks. We couldn't possibly be recognized.

We reached the entanglements and stopped, hugging the

ground. The sky was lit up by a far-off flare, and I could make out the wall of the trench, beyond the entanglements, and, in the wall, the loopholes, like black spots. To avoid a shot from a lookout who was shooting in front of us, I had veered slightly to the left. But the lookout was still so close to us that I could hear, after every shot, the casing of the expelled cartridge hit the trench wall and bounce down to the ground, onto the rocks.

We started sliding the tube under the entanglement when, twenty or thirty meters to our right, the darkness of the night was broken by a flash of light, accompanied by a shattering explosion. The first gelignite tube had been set off. I looked at my watch; its phosphorescent hands were showing three o'clock. That must have been Santini's tube. We had agreed that the first tube, whether it was his or mine, wasn't to be exploded before three. He'd been more precise than I had. A shower of shards and stones radiated out all around us. We hugged the ground even tighter.

A couple of dozen rockets shot into the air all down the line, even beyond our front line, and the machine guns opened fire. The alarm had been sounded now.

A second explosion followed the first, and a third came immediately after. The rockets multiplied, chaotically zigzagging across the sky in every conceivable direction. The lookout closest to us didn't lose his cool. He didn't shout out any alarms and just kept on shooting, calmly, as before. He must have been a veteran, too. But further to the right, the rifle and machine-gun fire was furious. The troops must have rushed up to the front line.

Uncle Francesco gave no signs of life, but I still felt his presence, and the muffled smell of his cigar was still wafting my way. He had lit it before leaving the trench, and kept the lit end inside his mouth. That way the cigar smoke was hidden and it lasted longer. He would use it to light the fuse on the tube. I turned my head and got a glimpse of him close by, lying on his back, looking up at the sky, the cigar in his mouth. He must have been enjoying the pyrotechnic spectacle that the Austrians were offering us for free. Surely he hadn't seen anything better at the feast of the patron saint in his little village. And I, too, just then, saw the whole sky lit up by rockets. It looked as though all those fireworks, exploding over that forest of fir trees, were lighting up the columns and the naves of an immense basilica.

Our tube had passed under the entanglements. I took advantage of the first bit of darkness that fell over us and slithered backward to leave room for Uncle Francesco. Using his cigar, he lit the fuse and covered it with a rock. Together we took cover behind the trunk of a fir tree and waited for the explosion.

A half hour later we were back in our trench. The ten tubes had all gone off. We called the roll; nobody was missing. Only one soldier from Santini's group had been wounded, in the leg.

Before going back to their units, the soldiers finished off the brandy that was their reward for volunteering.

XII

The next day, the 1st Battalion launched the assault. The Austrians, alerted by the explosions during the night, were waiting for them. The machine guns mowed down the first waves and the battalion didn't even make it as far as the trenches. The whole day long, up and down the length of the narrow valley, all we could hear were the cries and moaning of the wounded.

Without artillery, it was pointless to think of taking such strongly defended positions. The 2nd Battalion tried another assault, but it was futile, too. Everybody began to lose heart. The troops looked on the arrival of new gelignite tubes with terror. The tubes at night meant an assault the next day. Those were dismal days.

To lull the enemy into a false sense of security, tubes were exploded every night for a week without being followed by an attack the next day. Our commanders figured that once the barbed wire was destroyed we could finally launch a surprise attack. But the repetitious tube operation resulted in a lot of casualties, and fewer soldiers volunteered. In the end, the squads had to be ordered to take turns. Uncle Francesco was still unhurt and still a volunteer. But one night he didn't come back either. Later, his tube-mate carried his dead body back to the trench. The deposit slips of his earnings were found in the company's administrative office. After every mission he sent his ten-lire reward home to his family. Poor Uncle Francesco! His veteran comrades obtained permission to accompany his remains to the cemetery in Gallio, and I was among them. There were so few of us left! The Carso brigade was dwindling away on the high plateau of Asiago.

The battalion's most senior officer, the newly arrived Captain Bravini, took over the command. A young career officer, he did everything he could to get the battalion back in order. After two days, he was drinking brandy, too; first in secret and then openly. And he ended up hunting for my ration as though it were a buried treasure.

Eventually, all those exploded gelignite tubes called for an assault. Right around that time, Major Carriera, commander of our regiment's 2nd Battalion, had been promoted to lieutenant colonel. He was assigned the task of directing the assault in our sector. My battalion was also placed under his command for the operation. He was a man who was willing to do anything. General Leone held him in the highest esteem. And he, in turn, esteemed the general. The two of them were made for each other. From the moment he was assigned to direct the assault he didn't shut an eye day or night. He wanted to set an example. He was indefatigable. After a sleepless night, the next morning he did an hour of Swedish calisthenics and insisted that his adjutant do them, too. With his weak physical constitution, the adjutant almost got sick from the fatigue.

The lieutenant colonel had the following plan: At night, set off the tubes; at dawn, send out scouts and have them use wire cutters to widen the breaches in the barbed wire; immediately afterward, assault. So he had come up with the new variation of the wire cutters. Talk of them made my hair stand on end. On the Carso, we had lost our best soldiers under the enemy's barbed-wire entanglements thanks to these things. Captain Bravini, lower in rank than the lieutenant colonel but like him a battalion commander, did everything the lieutenant colonel told him to do, without objection. I hid my battalion's wire cutters. At dawn, the lieutenant colonel called for them and Captain Bravini looked for them in vain. So we were forced to give up on them.

The lieutenant colonel called his adjutant and asked him, "Do we still have wire cutters in the Second Battalion?"

I was hoping he would say no because I had told him what to expect. He had been on the Carso, too, and he knew what came from using wire cutters. The lieutenant adjutant reflected for a moment and responded, "Yes, sir, we do, we still have seven pair, of which five are in excellent condition. Three large and two small."

But he was bothered by a doubt. He pulled a notepad out of his pocket and corrected himself. "Of which four are in excellent condition. Two large and two small."

He taught Greek in a high school near Bologna and he was always precise, even with the most seemingly insignificant details.

I was standing next to him and said to him under my

breath, with disdain, "You're going to have a great career with your wire cutters."

"I do my duty," he replied calmly.

The wire cutters, all seven pair, were brought in shortly. The light of dawn was beginning to poke through the darkness in the woods, but so tenuously that we could barely even see one another.

"Captain," the lieutenant colonel ordered my battalion commander, "send out an officer and two soldiers to reconnoiter the barbed wire and use the wire cutters to widen the breaches for the attack."

The captain ordered Lieutenant Avellini, from the 9th Company, to go out with two soldiers. The young lieutenant was a career officer who had just arrived in the battalion a few days before. He presented himself, listened to the orders, and didn't say a word. He took the wire cutters, distributed a pair to each soldier, and disappeared, followed by the two men.

Several minutes went by without the slightest sound. The rifle fire from the lookouts continued per routine. I made some observations to Captain Bravini. "Our guys are going to need some light to be able to see the entanglements and cut the wire. And if there's light, the Austrians will be able to see, too, and shoot at our guys. We should make sure the enemy trenches are empty."

The captain was nervous. He didn't speak. He was worried about the operation, too. He'd already drunk half a canteen of brandy.

Two shots rang out from the enemy trench. They weren't

from the lookouts. More shots followed and then the whole line opened fire. Our guys had been spotted. We couldn't see very clearly from our trench.

"There's no doubt," Captain Bravini muttered, "that the Austrians are shooting at our guys. Operations like this can only be done at night, in the dark. But at night you can't see. So you can't do them at night or during the day. You have to have artillery. Without artillery you can't advance." The captain repeated, "You have to have artillery." And he couldn't pull himself away from his canteen.

The lieutenant colonel was nervous too. He was pacing back and forth in the trench, not saying a word. His adjutant followed behind him, he too back and forth, like a shadow.

From the loopholes, two steps away from our trench, we saw Lieutenant Avellini and a soldier pop up from behind some bushes. We threw some sandbags down on the ground and helped them climb back in. The soldier had a leg wound. The lieutenant's battle jacket had been shot clear through in several places around his hips but without leaving so much as scratch. He gave his report to the lieutenant colonel. The other soldier had been killed under the barbed wire. During the night, the Austrians had set up more chevaux-de-frise to reinforce the places where the barbed wire had been breached by the tubes. A few places along their line could be crossed, but only one man at a time. The Austrians had sounded the alarm. The wire cutters didn't cut.

Lieutenant Avellini was still holding his wire cutters and gave them to the lieutenant colonel. There were rolls of barbed wire in our trench. He took one end of a roll and clamped the wire cutters on it. The blades of the cutters slipped over the wire without making a dent. Despite all his Swedish calisthenics, his body was awkward and clumsy and it was all he could do not to hurt himself. He tried over and over again, but to no avail. The wire remained intact and the wire cutters fell out of his hand.

The Greek professor picked up a pair of wire cutters that had been left on the ground, one of the seven, and tried it on the wire. This pair cut.

"But this one cuts perfectly," he said triumphantly to the lieutenant colonel.

"It cuts?" the other one asked.

"Yes, colonel, it cuts."

And for the second time, he offered us a demonstration of his discovery.

"Well, then," said the lieutenant colonel, "we have to keep trying."

"But this is not about wire cutters," I said, putting myself beside the captain and addressing myself to him. "Even if all the wire cutters worked and even if they were the best wire cutters in the whole army, the situation would still be the same. The Austrians will wait for us at the breaches and fire away, point blank, at anyone who comes near the barbed wire, with wire cutters or without."

"I'm in command here," said the colonel, "and I didn't ask for your opinion."

My captain didn't speak and I didn't respond.

The lieutenant colonel asked Captain Bravini for the name of another officer from the battalion to send out under the barbed wire.

Without a moment's hesitation, the captain suggested Lieutenant Santini and added that no one knew the terrain as well as he did. He sent an orderly to fetch him. By now, the morning light had gotten brighter and we could make out the whole profile of the enemy trenches. It didn't take much to understand that Santini was being sent to die pointlessly.

I raised another objection. "Now there's too much light," I said. "Besides, Santini already went out last night, with the tubes. Couldn't we put this off until dawn tomorrow?"

My captain didn't dare say a word. The lieutenant colonel looked at me hostilely and said, "Stand at attention and be quiet!"

The Greek professor continued making the rounds to show everybody, all the nearby officers and soldiers, that the wire cutters were in excellent condition.

Lieutenant Santini arrived, followed by his orderly. The lieutenant colonel explained what was wanted of him and asked if he wished to volunteer. He was brave and had too much pride, and I was afraid he was going to answer yes. I moved up close behind him and, pulling on the tails of his jacket, whispered to his back, "Say no."

"It's an impossible operation," Santini replied. "And too late."

"I didn't ask you," the lieutenant colonel rebutted, "if it's early or late. I asked if you wanted to volunteer."

I pulled on the tails of his jacket again.

"No, sir," Santini replied.

The lieutenant colonel looked at Santini almost as though he couldn't believe his ears, looked at Captain Bravini, looked at me, looked at the whole group of nearby officers and soldiers who were leaning against the wall of the trench, and exclaimed, "This is cowardice!"

"You asked me a question, and I gave you my answer. It's not a matter of cowardice or bravery."

"You do not wish to volunteer?" the lieutenant colonel asked.

"No, sir."

"Well, then, I order you, I say I order you, to go out there anyway, immediately." The lieutenant colonel spoke calmly; his voice had the sound of a kind request, almost suppliant. But the look on his face was stern.

"Yes, sir," Santini replied. "If you give me an order, I cannot but obey it."

"But an order like that cannot be obeyed," I said to the captain, hoping he would intervene. But he remained silent.

"Get the wire cutters," the lieutenant colonel ordered, with a kind voice and cold eyes.

The adjutant came over with the wire cutters. He passed right by me. I couldn't contain myself and I shouted at him, "You could go out there yourself with those goddamn wire cutters of yours."

The lieutenant colonel heard me but responded to Santini. "So move out, lieutenant," he ordered.

"Yes, sir," said Santini.

He took the wire cutters. He unlatched from his belt a Viennese dagger made from a deer horn, a trophy of war, and handed it to me.

"Keep this in my memory," he said.

He was white as a sheet. He pulled out his pistol and climbed up out of the trench. The orderly, whom none of us had noticed since he'd arrived in the company of the lieutenant, grabbed a pair of wire cutters and climbed out of the trench.

I was still holding the dagger. Captain Bravini was sucking on his canteen. I ran over to the nearest loophole and saw the two of them, straight up on their feet, one beside the other, proceeding, in step, toward the enemy trenches. It was already full daylight.

The Austrians didn't open fire. Yet the two of them were moving forward out in the open. At that point there were no more than fifty meters between our trenches and the enemy's. There were only a few trees and the bushes were low. If they had thrown themselves on the ground, under the bushes, they could have made it unseen, at least as far as the barbed wire. Santini put his pistol back in his holster and moved forward, with only the wire cutters in hand. His orderly was still right beside him, with his rifle and wire cutters. They moved across the short space and stopped in front of the barbed wire. No shots came from the trenches. My heart was beating like a hammer. I raised my head from the loophole and looked at our trench. Everyone was at the loopholes.

How long did they stand there in front of the barbed wire? I have no recollection of it.

Finally, Santini gestured repeatedly with his hand toward his companion to get him to go back. Maybe he thought he could save him. But it was the weary gesture of a disheartened man. The soldier remained at his side.

Santini got down on his knees next to the barbed wire and started cutting it. The orderly did the same. It was then that a volley of rifle fire rang out from the enemy trench. The two of them collapsed to the ground.

From our trenches, machine-gun and rifle fire, as rabid as it was vain, responded in reprisal. I pulled myself away from the loophole and went looking for the Greek professor. I lit into him.

"Now that you've completed such a successful operation, you can go eat, fully satisfied."

He didn't answer me, and looked at me with pain. He had tears in his eyes. But I was too upset to contain myself.

"Now, you and your strategist have the duty to go out, both of you on patrol, with your wire cutters and carry on with the work that Santini and his orderly have left unfinished."

"If they order me to go out," he replied, "I'll go out immediately."

The lieutenant colonel was planning the assault by the two battalions for eight o'clock. The regiment commander and the brigade commander came to the line and made him call it off.

That night the details arrived with more tubes and brandy. So the operation would be launched again. Our pursuit would continue.

XIII

Following another assault by the 1st Battalion, launched and repelled, we had a few days' respite, which, on both sides of the line, was spent reinforcing the trenches. By now it was mid-July. Our artillery was starting to make its entrance onto the high plateau. A motorized battery made an appearance on the Gallio road, fired off a hundred or so grenades, which fell on our troops, and vanished. That was the last we ever saw or heard of it. The soldiers dubbed it the "phantom battery." That same day, the enemy artillery responded in reprisal against our lines and our brigade commander was seriously wounded.

More replacements arrived and my battalion was restored to full strength. Each company had a captain and four subordinate officers. Captain Bravini, commander of the 10th Company and the most senior officer, continued to serve as interim battalion commander until the arrival of a higher-ranking officer.

The army corps on either side of ours had also suffered serious losses in stalemates on Mount Interrotto, Mount Colombella, Mount Zingarella, and beyond. Ours was not the only division in action; the operation involved the entire army of the high plateau. The idea of the pursuit, which General Leone had made his own in a special way, was a directive from the Supreme Command.

News of the arrival of another group of batteries came in the midst of more preparations for another assault. My battalion was notified that it would be the first to attack and received orders to send out new reconnaissance patrols. But the exact day for the attack had not yet been decided.

It was now, as I recall, July 16. I had received orders to accompany the commander of the 9th to the front line and to give him all necessary clarifications so he could get to know the terrain and the positions of the enemy lines. He had arrived the day Santini died and he, too, had watched, from the loopholes of our trench, as he was killed. He had been deeply affected by it. The battalion commander had established a new attack order for the companies; in the next operation, the 9th was to take the lead. Its commander, therefore, had to know, in all of its parts, the sector in which he would soon be called to act.

I found him at his company command, which was behind the first line of support. He was drinking and he seemed to be in a good mood. He too had heard about the preparations for the next operation. I communicated the dispositions of the battalion commander.

"I know, sure, I know," he told me, "now it's my turn to lead the way. One at a time, they get us all killed."

"This time we'll have artillery," I said, to lift his spirits.

"We'll have the enemy artillery," the captain shot back.

"The barbed wire is everywhere. It's totally useless for me to study the terrain. It makes no difference if we attack from the left or the right. And it doesn't matter to me whether I die on the right or on the left. But if that's what the battalion commander wants, then sure, let's go have a look."

It might have been five o'clock in the afternoon. My intention was to accompany him to the right, to the highest elevation point of our trenches. From there, we could view the entire terrain between our trenches and the enemy's, and we could get a clear view, looking left toward Mount Interrotto, of the arrangement of the barbed wire and the enemy trench at the point where the 9th was supposed to attack. It was the location of loophole 14, the best observation loophole in the entire sector. It had been built on a rock that stuck straight out, forming an acute angle, facing the enemy. That loophole was ill suited for the terrain in front of it and further off to the right toward Casara Zebio, but, as distant as it was, you could make out, in several points lower down and to the left, even the movement of the Austrian soldiers in their trenches and passageways. I had been there almost every day and I had also been able to make some relief drawings for the regiment command. That part of our trench was occupied by 12th Company.

We had already walked most of the line and were approaching the highest elevation when an officer from the 12th came to meet us. I asked him to take us to loophole 14.

"During the day it's closed," he replied. "It's not usable anymore. The Austrians have spotted it and they keep a mounted rifle trained on it. Yesterday we had a lookout killed, this morning one was wounded. The company commander ordered that it be closed with a rock during the day."

"Too bad," I said. "It would have been really useful for the captain here. We'll make do with the other ones."

"From the other loopholes," the officer pointed out, "you can't see all that much. But I've made a lot of sketches and the captain is welcome to see them. It's just like looking out from loophole fourteen."

"What do you mean, sketches?" the captain exclaimed. "I want to look through loophole fourteen."

"The company commander," the officer replied, "has expressly forbidden it."

"And I'm going to look anyway," the captain concluded.

He walked off through the trench, looking for the loophole by number. He went off on his own, taking long strides.

"Send someone to call the company commander," I told the officer. Otherwise, this guy, who's been drinking, is going to do something crazy."

A soldier was already on his way to the company command and we rushed ahead to catch up to the captain. We got to loophole 14 just as he did. The captain approached it; the loophole was covered by a rock. He reached out to move the rock.

"If the captain has given an order," I said, holding his arm back, "we have to respect it."

"And me, what am I? Aren't I a captain?" he rebuffed me in a tone of command.

It was a matter of a few seconds. The captain was standing in front of the loophole. With a swift move he removed the rock and looked. A rifle shot rang out and the captain fell to the ground. An exploding bullet had snapped his right jawbone in two, destroying most of it.

That night, coming back in from an inspection of the front line, I was taking Lieutenant Avellini, who had assumed command of the 9th after the captain was wounded, back to his company. There was a light shining from inside a wooden shelter, a lean-to, supported by a big rock. The shelter was protected on the sides by sandbags and only from up close could you see the light inside through some holes between the bags. I stopped and looked in. There was a lighted candle in the center of the room. Thirty or so soldiers were gathered around it, sitting or lying down, and smoking.

"Let's hear what they have to say about the captain's wound," I whispered to Avellini.

We moved closer and listened. Several of them were talking.

"Another assault tomorrow!"

"I bet tomorrow there'll be another assault."

"And why wouldn't there be? Aren't we cursed sons of bitches?"

"There's no way. The provision detail hasn't delivered any chocolate or brandy."

"It'll get here afterward, when we're all dead. And the quartermaster sergeant will hog it all for himself."

"No, I'm telling you. There's never been an attack without chocolate and brandy. The chocolate I suppose we could do without, but not the brandy."

"You'll see, these bastards are going to get us all killed, with no chocolate and no brandy."

"I think so, too. They like us hungry, thirsty, and desperate. That way, we've got no desire to live. For them, the more miserable we are the better. That way, it's all the same to us whether we're dead or alive."

"That's the way it is."

"That's exactly the way it is."

"Try to act a little less like a jackass. You eat like a vulture every day and then all you do is complain. Now your delicate little stomach needs some chocolate and some little chocolate candies. If you don't replace the two reserve cans of meat you ate, you'll see what happens to you. As squad commander I don't want any more headaches."

"And who pays you to spy on people?"

"If the captain hadn't gotten wounded today, he'd have had your stomach opened to pull the meat out of it."

"If there's no brandy, I'm not going on any assault."

"And where the hell do you think I'm going to find two cans of meat?"

"You'll go, even without the brandy. Just like you always have."

"Find them wherever you want, but find them. Steal them. You've gotten so fat you can't even steal things at night anymore."

"Two tanks of brandy. I saw them this morning."

"That wasn't brandy. It was benzene for the rifles. I pinched a mess tin of the stuff."

"All right, so I'm forced to go on the assault even without the brandy. If I don't go, they shoot me. But you do it for fun."

"They'll end up killing us all, with or without the brandy."

"Hey! They die, too. They say the general's wound is really bad."

"Too bad for him. Wasn't he paid to be a general?"

"Yeah, they die, too, but with all the comforts. Steak for breakfast, steak for lunch, steak for dinner."

"And with a monthly salary that would last my family two years."

"But you'll see, he's not going to die. Those people, not one of them ever dies for real."

"They live well even when they're dead."

"If they all died, we'd be better off, too."

"If they all died, the war would be over."

"We should kill them all."

"We couldn't even manage to kill the division commander. We're all a bunch of poor beggars. We're not good for anything."

"We're not good for anything."

"Nothing."

"Nothing."

"I hear the captain said, 'I'm not about to lead my soldiers to get themselves butchered like a bunch of chickens.' He preferred to get himself a bullet in the head."

"Who told you that?"

"They were saying it in the company, when they brought him by here on the stretcher."

"We should really kill them all, from the captain on up. Otherwise, for us, there's no way out of this."

"And the captain who's the battalion commander?"

"He's after a career just like the rest of them. But his day will come, too."

"They're all after a career. Their shoulder bars are made from dead bodies."

"They say Lieutenant Santini left a will."

"I heard that, too."

"Me, too."

"What does the will say? Was he married, the lieutenant?"

"What do you mean, married! His will said, 'I urge my dear soldiers to shoot them all, as soon as they can do it without risk to themselves. All of them, without exception.'"

"Now there was a man!"

"He wasn't afraid of anything."

"He was a poor beggar like the rest of us."

"The lieutenant platoon commander is sure not going to get himself killed for us. He's scared stiff."

"And you're not scared? You're saying you're not scared?"

"If I've got my brandy, I'm not scared of anything."

"If you weren't scared you'd have run away already."

"Run away? And where am I going to run to?

"Who's got a little brandy for me?"

"Brandy? Cartridges, if you like."

"Half a cigar for anyone who gives me some brandy."

"Let's see."

"Quiet! There's somebody outside."

"Here's your half a cigar."

"Quiet!"

We were right up against the shelter, on the back side. On the other side, at the entrance to the shelter, the company quartermaster looked in and shouted, "Five men on fatigue for the chocolate and brandy!"

"They fatten the pig well before killing it."

"They fatten it well!"

"They fatten us well!"

XIV

The division commander wanted to direct the preparations for the attack personally. From the very first hours of the morning he was on the front line, in the trenches occupied by my battalion. The regiment commander was with him. The general was used to having everything under his control. His indefatigable tenacity was every bit as intense as his fearlessness. This time, he was determined to break through.

Word had already started to spread during the night that a lot of different-caliber batteries would be collaborating in the operation. Finally, then, the artillery would destroy all those damn trenches and barbed wire for us! It was time. After the "phantom battery," no other batteries had been heard on the high plateau.

The pieces didn't arrive en masse. Nevertheless, General Leone decided to send us a sample of what we could expect. He had a 75mm cannon set up in our trench. Dragged in by the fatigue details over the mule trails and paths, the cannon got to the line just after the general. It was a piece of Déport field artillery, shielded. It presented itself all alone, as a decorous official representative of the artillery corps. Where its companions were none of us would ever know. They had probably also been sent, as special ambassadors, to the various brigades scattered over the high plateau. Their voices, however, never reached us.

The artillerymen and foot soldiers worked together to make a large opening in the wall of our trench and mounted the cannon there, its wheels outside, the carriage inside the trench. As soon as the Austrians saw it they opened fire. The piece, with its armored shields in front and on the sides, remained impassive to the shooting. The general gave an order and the second lieutenant of the artillery, who commanded the gun crew, gave the order to open fire.

The general, the colonel, Captain Bravini, and I were standing near the piece, sheltered by the trench. At the first blasts of the cannon, the general, without changing in the least the austere expression on his face, rubbed his hands together in satisfaction. He looked around at the soldiers, searching, with his hard stare, for consensus. He didn't speak, but his whole demeanor said, "Look at what your general has managed to bring you here on the front line." The soldiers remained indifferent, incapable of appreciating the gift.

From the very first blasts of the cannon, the machine-gun and rifle fire began to die down until it ceased altogether. It was replaced by a lone sharpshooter, opposite the cannon. With a very precise, increasingly precise, aim, he tried to hit the gunner of the piece through the little sight holes in the shield. All the crew members serving the piece, spurred by the rifle fire, stepped up the pace of the shelling. That little rifle shot, persistent but labored, was covered by the blasts of the cannon and by the shells exploding in the trench. The general kept on rubbing his hands.

"Bravo, lieutenant!" he said to the artilleryman. "Well done! Well done!"

From Val d'Assa, no less than seven kilometers away, an enemy battery of 152mm cannons fired some bracketing rounds at our 75mm piece. In a matter of seconds, a shower of grenades came raining down around us. The gun crew appeared not even to notice and remained fixed at their battle stations. Some grenades fell in front of our trenches without wounding anyone; others smashed into the enemy trenches. Our cannon had found itself a nice auxiliary. As though those rounds had been fired by our piece, the general cranked up his level of enthusiasm.

"Bravo, lieutenant!" he repeated. "I'm going to consider you for a special promotion for merit of war."

The lone sharpshooter was gradually honing in on his target. He was methodically refining his aim. A shot passed through the hole in the shield and fractured the arm of the gunner. Without saying a thing, he showed the lieutenant his wounded arm. The officer took his place and continued firing. The lone sharpshooter kept firing too.

The 152mm battery fell silent, evidently satisfied.

Our 75mm piece kept on firing, but its shots were now falling first on the barbed wire and then on the trenches with no effect. It seemed clear that it could keep on firing all day long with the same result.

The colonel, who until that moment had stood silently at the general's side, exclaimed, "All of this accomplishes nothing."

The general didn't get irritated. On the contrary, he seemed to pay heed to the colonel. "Do you really believe that this accomplishes nothing?"

"Nothing," the colonel replied, convinced. "Absolutely nothing, general."

I looked at him in amazement. It was the first time he had ever dared express a negative opinion to a superior.

The general reflected. He caressed his chin with the tip of his Alpine walking stick and stood there concentrating for a long time. He, too, must have noted that the 75mm was impotent against a trench dug into the ground and such an extensive line of barbed wire. While the general was reflecting, the lieutenant was wounded in the arm, too. A sergeant immediately took his place. The gun crew, moving mechanically, feverishly kept on serving the gun.

The lieutenant passed by the general, bandaging his arm. The general appeared to have made a decision. He gave him a pat on the back and told him to give the order to cease firing.

Then he turned to the colonel.

"Now we'll put the Farina body armor into action."

I looked at my watch. It was after eight o'clock.

A detail brought in eighteen Farina cuirasses. This was the first time I'd seen them. They were different from my major's cuirass, which was light, layered like fish scales, and covered only the torso and abdomen. These cuirasses were thick, in two or three pieces that protected the neck and the upper arms, and covered the whole body all the way down to the knees. They couldn't have weighed less than a hundred pounds. Every cuirass also had a helmet, it too very thick.

The general stood erect in front of the cuirasses. After the fleeting satisfaction he'd gotten from the first blasts of the cannon, he was again composed, immobile. Now he spoke scientifically.

"These are the famous Farina cuirasses," the general explained to us, "which are known only to the few. They are especially celebrated because they make it possible to carry out extremely risky operations in the full light of day. It's a shame there aren't more of them! In this entire army corps there are only eighteen of them. And they are ours! Ours!"

I was in the trench standing next to Captain Bravini. Next to me, but a few meters away, was a group of soldiers. The general spoke in a normal tone of voice. The soldiers heard him, too. One soldier commented under his breath, "I'd rather have a canteen of good brandy."

"We alone," the general continued, "have been granted the privilege of having them. No matter if the enemy has rifles, machine guns, cannons, the Farina cuirasses can go anywhere."

"Anywhere, in a manner of speaking," observed the colonel, who was in a heroic mood that day.

The fearsome general did not react and looked at him as though he had raised an objection of a technical nature. By temperament the colonel was slow and passive, but every once in a while he allowed himself some excesses that, from others, wouldn't have been tolerated. He had the physical stature of a giant and a huge family fortune—two imposing qualities.

"I've had some experience with the Farina cuirasses," the colonel explained, "and I can't say I have fond memories of them. But maybe these are better."

"Certainly, certainly, these are better," the general resumed. With these you can go anywhere. The Austrians . . ." The general lowered his voice, guardedly, and glanced over at the enemy trenches, to make sure he wasn't overheard. "The Austrians have spent enormous sums trying to uncover the secret, but they haven't succeeded. The captain from the Corps of Engineers who was shot in Bologna, they say he'd sold himself to the enemy for these cuirasses. But he was executed in time. My dear colonel, would you be so kind as to order the sapper unit into action?"

The sapper unit had been prepared the day before and was waiting to be deployed. They were volunteers from the pioneer unit, commanded by a sergeant, also a volunteer. In just a few minutes, they were in the trench, each with a pair of wire cutters. They put on the cuirasses in our presence. The general himself joined them and helped latch a few buckles.

"They look like medieval warriors," the general observed. The rest of us remained silent. The volunteers weren't smiling. They did everything in a rush and seemed determined. The other soldiers in the trench looked at them warily.

I looked on at what was happening with anxiety. I recalled the cuirass of the major on Mount Fior. Certainly these were much more solid and could provide much better protection.

But what would these armored sappers really be able to accomplish, even if they were able to get through the barbed wire and reach the trenches?

Next to the cannon, we opened up another breach in the trench wall. The volunteer sergeant saluted the general. He responded solemnly, standing straight at attention, his hand stiff against his helmet. The sergeant was the first to go out, followed by the others, slow from the weight of the steel, sure of themselves, but bent down to the ground because the helmet covered their heads but not their faces. The general remained at attention until the last volunteer had gone, and then said to the colonel, gravely, "The Romans won because of their armor."

An Austrian machine gun opened fire, raking down the line from the right. Immediately another opened fire from the left. I looked at the soldiers around me in the trench. Their faces were deformed in grimaces of pain. They understood what was happening. The Austrians had been lying in wait. The sappers were now caught in the crossfire of two machine guns.

"*Avanti!*" the sergeant shouted to the sappers, urging them onward.

One after another, all the armored sappers fell.

None of them reached the enemy barbed wire.

"*Avan . . .*" repeated the voice of the sergeant, who was lying wounded in front of the barbed wire.

The general didn't say a word. The soldiers from the battalion looked at each other in terror. Now, what was going to become of them? The colonel looked at the general and asked, "Are we still supposed to attack at nine o'clock?"

"Certainly," the general replied, as though he had foreseen that things would go exactly as they actually had. "At nine o'clock sharp my division attacks along the entire front."

Captain Bravini took me by the arm and said, "Now it's our turn!"

He uncorked his canteen, and I believe he drank it dry.

XV

The cannon had produced, as its only accomplishment, the wounds of the gunner and the lieutenant. All the sappers had fallen. But the assault had to be launched just the same. The general was still there, like an inquisitor, determined to witness, to the bitter end, the agony of the condemned. It was just a few minutes before nine o'clock.

The battalion was ready, the bayonets inserted. The 9th Company was amassed around the breach opened for the sappers. The 10th was right behind them. The other companies were all in closed ranks inside the trench and the passageways and behind the rocks to the rear of the trenches. You couldn't hear a whisper. The only things moving were the canteens of brandy. From the belt to the mouth, from the mouth to the belt, from the belt to the mouth without interruption, set in motion like shuttles on a giant loom.

Captain Bravini had his watch in his hand, and he was staring at it, following intensely the inexorable passing of the minutes. Without taking his eyes off the watch, he yelled, "Ready to attack!"

Then he yelled again, "Ready for the assault! Officers, at the head of your units!

The wounded sapper sergeant kept on shouting, "*Avan...*"

The eyes of the soldiers, wide open, looked for our eyes. The captain was still bent over his watch and the soldiers found only my eyes. I forced myself to smile and mime a few words on the edge of my lips; but those eyes, brimming with questions and anguish, frightened me.

Of all of war's moments, the one just before an assault was the most gruesome.

"Ready for the assault!" the captain repeated once more.

The assault! Where were we going? We were leaving our shelter and going outside. Where? The machine guns, all of them, lying on their cartridge-crammed bellies, were waiting for us. Anyone who hasn't experienced those few seconds has not known war.

The captain's words came crashing down like slamming shutters. The 9th was on its feet, but I couldn't see all of it, squashed against the walls of the trench. The 10th was on the other side of me, in the middle of the trench, and I could distinguish each of its soldiers. Two of the soldiers moved and I saw them, one beside the other, maneuvering their rifles into place under their chins. One of them bent over, fired his rifle, and slumped down on himself. The second soldier imitated the first and collapsed next to him. Was it cowardice, bravery, or madness? The first was a veteran of the Carso.

"Savoy!" yelled Captain Bravini.

"Savoy!" the troops responded.

And it was a yell that had the sound of a wailful lament and a desperate invocation. The 9th, Lieutenant Avellini in the lead, poured out of the breach and launched into the assault. The general and the colonel were at the loopholes.

When the head of the 10th got to the breach, we threw ourselves forward. The 10th, the 11th, and the 12th followed us in a rush. In a few seconds the whole battalion was in front of the enemy trenches.

Whether we had yelled or not, the enemy machine guns were waiting for us. As soon as we got beyond a strip of rocky terrain and began the descent toward the valley, out in the open, they opened fire. Our shouts were covered by their gun bursts. The terrain was so thickly traversed by hisses and explosions that it seemed to me there must have been ten machine guns firing on us. The soldiers who got hit fell to the ground heavily, as though they had been thrown from trees.

For a minute or so, I was overcome by a sort of mental torpor, and my whole body felt heavy and slow. Maybe I'm wounded, I thought. Yet I could feel that I wasn't wounded. The machine gun bullets whizzing by and the constant rush of the units on our heels woke me up. Instantly I regained consciousness of my situation. Not anger, not hate, as in a brawl, but utter calm, absolute, a sort of infinite weariness wrapped around my now lucid mind. Then even that weariness subsided and I was running again, fast.

I felt calm again and I could see everything around me. Officers and men were falling with their arms outstretched and, as they fell, their rifles were thrown through the air in front of them.

Captain Bravini never stopped yelling, "Savoy!"

A lieutenant from the 12th passed right by me. He was red in the face and had a musket in his hand. He was a republican and detested the monarchist attack yell. As he saw me he cried out, "Viva l'Italia!"

I had a walking stick in my hand. I raised it up high to respond to him, but wasn't able to pronounce a word. If we had been on level terrain none of us would have reached the enemy entanglements. The machine guns would have mowed us all down. But the terrain had a slight downward slope and it was covered with bushes and rocks. The machine guns had to adjust their aim constantly for elevation and their fire became less effective. Nevertheless, the assault waves grew thinner, and out of the thousand men in the battalion, there were very few left who were still on their feet and advancing. I looked toward the enemy trenches. Their defenders were not hidden behind the loopholes. They were all standing up and leaning out over the trenches. They felt secure. A lot of them were even standing on the parapets. They were all shooting at us, carefully taking aim, as though it were a drill on the parade ground.

I stumbled over the sergeant of the sappers. He was lying on his side, the cuirass wrapped around him, his helmet shot through from side to side. He had been hit in the head while urging his men forward, and he kept repeating the cry that had been cut off in his throat, in a pitiful singsong. "*Avan . . . avan. . .*"

Around him lay the bodies of three sappers, their armor ripped with gaping holes.

We were coming to the trenches. Captain Bravini fell, too, and I saw him, his arms open wide, plummet into a bush. I thought he was dead. But immediately afterward, I heard the cry "Savoy!" repeated over and over in a faint voice.

The battalion was supposed to attack on a front two hundred fifty to three hundred meters wide. But the downward slope of the terrain had inevitably pushed all of us, as we gradually moved forward, toward the same strip of terrain right in front of the enemy trenches, barely fifty meters wide. The remains of the battalion were all amassed at that point. The machine guns couldn't hit us anymore, but we provided the standing riflemen with a compact target. We were being shot at point blank.

Suddenly, the Austrians stopped shooting. I saw the ones who were in front of us, their eyes thrust open with a terrified look, almost as though it were they and not us who were under fire. One of them, who didn't have a rifle, cried out in Italian, "*Basta! Basta!*"

"*Basta!*" the others repeated from the parapets.

The one who was unarmed looked like a chaplain.

"Enough, brave soldiers, don't get yourselves killed like this!"

We came to a halt for an instant. We weren't shooting, they weren't shooting. The one who seemed to be a chaplain was leaning out so close to us that if I had reached out my arm I could have touched him. He had his eyes fixed on us, and I looked back at him.

From our trench a harsh voice cried out, "Forward! Men of my glorious division, forward! Forward, against the enemy!"

It was General Leone.

Lieutenant Avellini was a few meters away from me. We looked at each other. He said, "Let's go forward."

I repeated, "Let's go forward."

I wasn't holding a pistol but an Alpine walking stick. I didn't think of taking out my pistol. I threw my stick at the Austrians. One of them caught it in midair. Avellini had his pistol in his hand. He moved forward, trying to climb up onto a tree trunk that was lying on top of the barbed wire. It was the trunk of a fir tree that, eradicated by an artillery shell, had crashed onto the barbed wire. He climbed up on top of it and struggled to walk across it, as though he were on a gangplank. He fired his pistol and shouted to the soldiers, "So shoot! Fire!"

A few soldiers fired their guns.

"Forward! Forward!" the general yelled.

Avellini was walking across the trunk and it was all he could do to keep his balance. Behind him, two soldiers struggled to keep their feet. I had come to an entanglement where it seemed to me it was possible to get through. There was a narrow passage through the wire. I started in. But after a few steps I found my way blocked by a cheval-de-frise. It was impossible to go on. I turned around and saw some soldiers from the 10th, who had followed me. I stood there frozen. There was no shooting coming from the trenches. Through a large loophole directly ahead of me. I got a glimpse of a soldier's head. He was looking at me. All I could see were his eyes. And it seemed to me that all he had was eyes; they looked so big. Slowly, I took a few steps backward, without turning my back, still under the gaze of those big eyes. Then I thought, "the eyes of an ox."

I wiggled out of the entanglement and made my way toward Avellini. There was already a group of soldiers standing on the tree trunk, holding each other up. As I was approaching the trunk, a voice of command cried out from the enemy trench, "*Feuer!*"

Two shots rang out. The trunk turned over and the men fell on their backs. Avellini wasn't hit and he responded with two pistol shots. We all threw ourselves on the ground in the middle of some bushes, and took cover behind the fir trees. The assault was over. It's taken me a long time to describe it but the whole thing couldn't have lasted more than a minute.

Avellini was nearby and he whispered to me, "What should we do?"

"Stay put and wait until it gets dark," I replied.

"And the assault?" he insisted.

"The assault?"

The Austrians kept shooting, but their aim was high. We were safe. We could still hear Captain Bravini's weary voice, feeble. He kept on repeating "Savoy." On all fours, I went looking for the captain. I think it took me an hour to get to him. He was lying down, his head behind a rock, one hand on his head. His jacket was off and one arm was bandaged and covered with blood. Around him there were only dead bodies. He must have bandaged himself. The bushes kept him hidden from the trenches. I got very close to him without him noticing. I touched him on the leg and he saw me. He took a long look at me and repeated again, lowering his voice, "Savoy."

I held my finger up to my lips to tell him to keep quiet. I crawled over to his head and whispered in his ear, "Shut up!"

He seemed to wake up from a long sleep. He put his finger up to his lips, too, and didn't talk anymore. It was as though I had pushed the button of a mechanical device and turned it off.

Now the whole valley was quiet. Our wounded had stopped their crying. The sapper sergeant had gone quiet, too, dropped off into eternal silence. Even the Austrians weren't shooting anymore. The sun was shining on the little battlefield. The rest of the day went by like that, an instant and an eternity.

When, after dark, we returned to our lines, the general was there to shake the hands of all the officers—five, counting the wounded. As he took his leave, he said to Captain Bravini, who had a fractured forearm, "You can count on a Silver Medal for Military Valor."

The captain remained at attention until the general had disappeared. Left alone with us, he sat down and cried all night, without managing to say a word.

When we had finished carrying back the wounded and the dead, which the Austrians allowed us to gather without firing a shot, I lay down and tried to get to sleep. My head was so light it felt like I was breathing with my brain. I was exhausted but I couldn't get to sleep. The Greek professor came over to talk. He was depressed. His battalion had been part of the assault as well, farther to the left, and had been destroyed, like ours. He talked to me with his eyes closed.

"I'm afraid of going crazy," he told me. "I'm going to go crazy one of these days, or I'm going to kill myself. I've got to kill myself."

I didn't know what to say. I, too, could feel the ebb and flow of waves of madness. At times, I could feel my brain sloshing around inside my skull, like water inside a shaken bottle.

XVI

General Leone was nervous as a cat. He had been cited in the army's daily order and this distinction rekindled his desire for daring deeds. He showed up on the front line day and night. He was clearly pondering new exploits. But the brigade's losses were too great and it couldn't be put into action again until it was reconstituted. In my battalion, we had only two hundred men left, including Ottolenghi's machine-gun section, which had stayed behind during the assault to defend our trenches. We were down to three officers. Captain Bravini, whose fractured arm had been labeled a flesh wound, died a few days later. Another officer, wounded in the foot, had to be hospitalized for surgery.

The end of July and the first fifteen days of August were a nice long rest for us, not a single assault in those days. Life in the trenches, though hard, is nothing compared to an assault. The assault is what makes war a calamity. For a soldier, death is a normal event and you are not afraid to die. But the awareness of imminent death, the certainty that death is inevitable, makes the hours leading up to the assault a tragedy. Why did those two soldiers of the 10th kill themselves? In the normal life of the trenches nobody foresees their death or believes it is inevitable; and it arrives unannounced, sudden and mild. In any big city, after all, there are far more accidental deaths than there are in an army trench. Even the discomforts you get used to. Even the most feared contagious diseases. Like cholera, what's that? Nothing. We had outbreaks of it in the First and Second Armies, with a lot of deaths, and the troops laughed it off. What's cholera compared to being caught in an enfilade of machine-gun fire?

Those days of relaxed life in the trenches were even fun.

The men sat in the shade singing songs, read a hundred times the letters they'd received from home, made engravings on the copper bracelets they'd pulled off grenades, picked the fleas off their bodies, and smoked.

Every once in a while a newspaper happened our way and we passed it around among ourselves. They were always the same and they annoyed us. The way they described the war was so strange it was unrecognizable. The Campomulo valley, which, after Mount Fior, we had crossed without seeing a single casualty, was depicted in the papers as "lined with cadavers." Austrian cadavers, naturally. There was always music blaring before our assaults, which were described as a delirium of song and conquest. Even our little army newspapers were irritating. The truth was something only we possessed, right before our eyes.

One day, Second Lieutenant Montanelli came to see me. He was a veteran from the 2nd Battalion, in command of a pioneer unit. He was an engineering student at the University of Bologna and we'd known each other since serving on the

Carso. He, too, was one of the few survivors of the fighting on the high plateau. He arrived as I was reading.

"You read?" he said to me. "Aren't you ashamed of yourself?"

"And why shouldn't I read?" I replied.

He was wearing a raincoat, all buttoned up. All you could see of his clothing were his helmet, the raincoat, the lower half of his gaiters, and his shoes, falling apart and held together by tangled pieces of wire. The soles were new, made out of pine bark. He unbuttoned his raincoat and exhibited his bare naked body, from his helmet to his gaiters. Two months of campaigning had left him in this state. Not a single piece of clothing had made it to the line since the end of May. We were all, some more, some less, dressed like hobos.

"Where's your underwear?" I asked.

"Not being an item of primary need I have abolished it. My bodily fauna was forcing me to undertake such strenuous hunting expeditions, for big game and small, that I preferred to burn their dens. Now I feel more like a man. I mean, more like an animal. And you read? I feel sorry for you. The life of the spirit? Don't make me laugh, the spirit. The spirit! We want to live, live, live."

"Where is it written that in order to live you have to abolish the shirt?"

"Drink and live. Brandy. Sleep and live and brandy. Stay in the shade and live. And still more brandy. And not think about anything. Because if we ever really thought about something we'd have to kill each other and put an end to it once and for all. And you read?"

I had come across some abandoned books in Villa Rossi, a house in the woods, about halfway on the road from Gallio to Asiago. It was a nighttime patrol incursion and didn't give me much time. In the rush, I chose *Orlando Furioso* by Ariosto, a book on birds, and a French edition of *The Flowers of Evil* by Baudelaire. The first few pages of the book on birds were missing and I never learned the name of the author. I took those books with me to the high plateau. Saved from destruction once by me and once by my orderly, I always kept them with me. It's very likely that this was the only mobile literary library in the entire army. My orderly had a special passion for birds, and that book, with its illustrations, was his pastime. He was a hunter. He barely knew how to read, but he was mostly interested in the pictures. Whenever I read he read, too, and we exchanged our impressions.

"Did you learn anything new?" I would ask him.

"The book is interesting. *Bertoldo and Bertoldino* was funnier but this one is prettier and more varied. All the birds are in here. There's not one that's missing. It even has fig peckers. I like eating all those little birds with polenta, don't get me wrong. Fig peckers are tasty. But, no offense to the Veneto, I prefer roasted blackbirds and thrushes."

I'd say to him, "I understand the thrushes come here from Germany, but not all of them."

"They can come from wherever they want; on the spit they're all the same. Not a bad one among them. But take it from me, lieutenant, sir, thrushes are exquisite if the spit is made of wood. Never, for the life of me, never commit the imprudence of using a metal spit. And never use the same spit twice. Every thrush wants its own spit. Be careful; you have to use soft wood. First, taste the wood. Chew on it a little and check the flavor. That's what I always do . . ."

Since in our idle hours my orderly always claimed the bird book, I was left with *Orlando* and *The Flowers of Evil*. But that was plenty. Without a doubt, the two of us were the only avid readers on the high plateau.

It was on the mountains of Asiago that I came to know two of the most characteristic spirits of Western culture. I already knew about them, but superficially, as one can get to know them by reading them at a desk in the city in normal times. I had no special memories of them. If you read at war, during rest periods, they are completely different. Ariosto was a little like our war correspondents; he wrote about a hundred battles without ever seeing even one. But what grace and what joy in the world of his heroes! Deep down, certainly, he was a skeptic, but he was compelled toward optimism. He is the genius of optimism. For him, all the great battles are pleasant excursions into the flowery countryside, and even death seems to be a congenial continuation of life. Some of his captains die, but they go on fighting without realizing they are dead.

Baudelaire is the opposite. The sun on the high plateau was made to light up his gloomy life. Like the student from Bologna, he could have roamed naked on the mountaintops drinking sunlight and brandy. He could well have fought in the war alongside the lieutenant colonel in the observation post in Stoccaredo. Like him, like a thousand others of my comrades,

Baudelaire needed to drink in order to numb his brain and forget. Life for him was what the war was for us. But what sparks of human joy gush forth from his pessimism!

It was a sunny day; the whole front was calm. Every once in a while, carried by the wind, the sound of a rifle shot reached our ears from Val d'Assa. My orderly, his rifle held between his knees like a spit, was bent over his birds. I was sitting next to him, with Angelica and Orlando, in flight. A merry voice interrupted our silence.

"Good morning, dear colleague!"

It was a lieutenant in the cavalry. I closed my book and stood up. We shook hands and introduced ourselves. He was from the Royal Piedmont regiment. On the staff of the army command, he was coming to the front line for the first time. He had never seen a trench before. Even now, he hadn't come on official business, but for his personal enjoyment, to get an idea of what the front line and our lives were like. Accompanied by an orderly from the regiment command, he was elegantly dressed, impeccable: white gloves, whip, yellow riding boots, and spurs.

I told him right off, "Be careful, because this flashy garb of yours will make you the target of all the sharpshooters on the other side."

He made a funny comment about the sharpshooters, and a funny comment about my book. He wanted to know the author. He confessed he had never read Ariosto.

I handed the book to the orderly, picked up my walking stick, and came back over to him. To resume the conversation, I said, "Orlando is divine."

"He certainly deserves," he replied, "to become president of the Council of Ministers."

"President of the council," I objected, "might be overdoing it. But he'd certainly be no worse at commanding the army than General Cadorna."

"No, His Excellency doesn't have the military training, but he is certainly the greatest orator and the greatest politician in the Parliament."

"His Excellency?"

The question grew complicated. In the brief clarification that followed, I realized that I had been talking about Orlando, the "Furioso," Ariosto's Orlando, while my colleague meant the Honorable Orlando, member of Parliament and Minister of Justice in the Boselli government. The lieutenant, like the minister, was Sicilian and had a boundless admiration for him. He eased his way out of the embarrassment with nonchalance. But the misunderstanding certainly inflated my pride as an infantry officer. The cavalry lieutenant's accent was amusing, too. He spoke with grace, and with more than a little affectation, almost suppressing the "r" in the French way, as we are used to hearing only from our cinema artists.

Actually, for a moment the embarrassment was more mine than his. He was so well dressed and all I had was my uniform, part shreds and part patches. Yes, I was an officer in a celebrated brigade, and he was a lancer in a reserve regiment, and what's more, on duty at the army command—not exactly near the front line. But I was indecent. It made me feel somehow like I was in the presence of a superior. Little by little, I reacted and managed to overcome the inferiority that a dirty man feels in front of a clean one. In almost no time we became good comrades.

I led the way and we went up into the trench. He wasn't afraid and, something that's always very dangerous in a trench, he wanted to show he wasn't afraid. I kept saying to him, "Do what I do," "Here, bend down," "Here, touch the ground with your hands," "Stop here," and he didn't bend down, didn't touch the ground, didn't stop. He wanted to look everywhere, inside the loopholes, on top of the parapets. I had a hard time convincing him to be cautious. Luckily, nobody took a shot at him.

We stopped in a corner to get out of the sun.

He said to me, "I think you foot soldiers are too cautious. Wars are not won with caution."

It was undoubtedly an ill-timed observation. I felt cut to the quick. An offense to my esprit de corps, that lesson of his seemed truly out of place.

"It's just that we can only count on our own two legs," I retorted. "In a difficult moment a foot soldier's knees might start shaking. If his knees are shaking he can't take a single step forward. You're much luckier. You can even be scared to death and your horse's legs will carry you forward just the same."

Afterwards, I regretted what I had said, but right then it was satisfying. It seemed to me that the cavalryman had it coming. He didn't respond.

We approached loophole 14.

"This," I explained, "is the best loophole in the sector, but it's only used at night, when the Austrians fire their rockets. During the day, it's forbidden to look through it. Several officers and soldiers have been killed or wounded here. The enemy has a tripod rifle trained on it that's constantly manned by a sharpshooter. The soldiers amuse themselves by holding up pieces of wood or paper in front of it, or coins on the end of a stick, and the sharpshooter never fails to thread the loophole and hit the target."

We both looked at the loophole. It was no longer, as it used to be, a hole in the wall closed by a rock. The soldiers had installed a shielded loophole there that they'd found in the ruins of Asiago. It was a heavy steel plate with an observation hole that could be opened and closed by moving a little shutter, also made of steel. I raised the shutter, keeping my body to the side, and waited for the shot. But the sharpshooter didn't fire.

"The lookout is asleep," the lieutenant said.

I let the shutter fall back into place over the hole and then raised it again. The sunlight shone through the hole like the luminous strip of a reflector. A hissing sound whizzed through the air, accompanied by a rifle blast. The bullet came right through the hole.

The lieutenant wanted to try it, too. He raised the shutter and put the end of his whip in front of the hole. Another shot rang out and the end of the whip was severed. He laughed. He picked up a piece of wood, stuck a coin on the end of it, and repeated the experiment again.

The coin, struck right in the center, was blown off the stick and whistled through the air.

"Tonight I'll have something to recount to the army command."

I moved on and pointed out the next loophole.

"From here," I said, "you can see another sector that's less important. Here there's no danger. You see, way down there, a pile that looks like a bag of coal? It's camouflage for a machine gun. We spotted it a few nights ago, when it started firing during an alarm. We've already informed regiment command about it, because if we launch another assault, it'll have to be destroyed by a light mountain gun."

"Do you have artillery now?"

"Yes, a few pieces. It's starting to be brought in. You see there, off to the right? It looks like a white dog. It's an observatory that dominates the other sector. And there, where you can see a thick pine grove, there's a gully. There the line is interrupted, and it starts up again on the other side, beyond the gully.

I was sure that he was looking out too, behind me. The loophole was big, and there was room for two. Then I heard his voice, a little ways off, as he said, "The legs of an officer in the Royal Piedmont shake less than the legs of his horse."

A rifle shot came on the heels of his words. I turned around. The lieutenant was standing at loophole 14 and crumbling to the ground. I rushed over to hold him up, but he was already dead. The bullet had struck him in the forehead.

XVII

With the middle of August came talk of another operation. The battalions had been brought back up to strength. Some field and mountain artillery batteries had already taken up positions in the army corps sector. On the line we weren't sleeping at night anymore. Patrols and gelignite tubes were on the move again. One day, an assault was announced for the next day, but it was postponed. So we were able to count on one more day of assured life. Anyone who hasn't fought in a war, in the conditions that we were fighting in, can't appreciate what that meant. In those conditions even a single hour of safety was a lot. To be able to say, at dawn, an hour before the assault, "I'm going to sleep another half hour, I can still sleep for a half hour, and then I'll get up and I'll smoke myself a cigarette, I'll warm up with a cup of coffee, I'll nurse it sip by sip, and then I'll smoke myself another cigarette," seemed like a pleasant plan for a whole lifetime.

The orders to get ready for a new battle coincided with the news that two regiments of the brigade had been granted the privilege of decorating their flags with the Gold Medal for Military Valor. This extraordinary honor, which distinguished us once again among all the infantry brigades, would have been appreciated by all of us if we had been at rest. The brigade commander wanted to celebrate the event in any case and summoned all the officers to report. In a short speech, he recalled the history of the brigade and ordered the company commanders to commemorate it in their units.

I was with the officers from my battalion. After the report, which took place at the brigade command, we went back to the line together. Behind us were the officers of the 1st Battalion, commanded by Captain Zavattari. He had been transferred from the 2nd Battalion to the 1st after the death of the major, and had assumed the command. My battalion was in the trench and the 1st was on the second line. To get back to the front line we had to pass by the 1st Battalion command.

We had gotten as far as the command when news came that General Leone was dead, struck in the chest by an exploding bullet. Why not call things by their real name? The news was greeted with jubilation, exaltation. Captain Zavattari invited us to stop in at his command and popped the corks of several bottles. Glass in hand, he made a toast.

"Fellow officers! Permission be granted to a representative of the Ministry of Public Instruction and to a veteran captain to raise a glass to the good fortune of our army. Imitating the beautiful traditions of those strong peoples who celebrate the death of a family member with banquets and dances, let us, unable to do better, drink to the memory of our general. No tears, oh gentlemen, but joy, opportunely restrained. The hand of God has touched the high plateau of Asiago. Without wishing to criticize the delay with which Providence enacts its will, we must nevertheless affirm that it was time. He has departed. Peace be with him. Peace with him and joy with us. And finally, let us be permitted to respect after his death a general we detested during his life."

We all had our glasses raised when, along the mule trail coming from Croce Sant'Antonio, an officer on horseback appeared amid the pine trees. I was standing across from the mule trail and saw him first. He was coming toward us. I cried out, "But it's not possible!"

We all looked. It was General Leone. On a mule, his helmet down over his eyes, his Alpine walking stick across his saddlebow, his binoculars around his neck, his face dark, he was coming toward us at a trot.

"Officers, at-ten-tion!" the captain cried out.

Without taking the time to put our glasses down, we all stood at attention. The captain, too, stiffened into a salute, his glass in hand.

"What blissful event are you celebrating?" asked the general gruffly. Everyone was overcome with embarrassment.

The captain pulled himself together and responded in a voice that sounded as though it came from beyond the tomb, "The Gold Medals for Military Valor awarded to our flags."

"Do I have your permission to toast with you?" the general asked.

The captain offered him his own glass, still intact. The general gulped it down, returned the empty glass, kicked his mule, and trotted off.

The next day was the day of the operation, supported by artillery. Two field artillery batteries opened breaches in the barbed-wire entanglements, throwing a section of the enemy trenches into disarray, enabling two companies of the 1st Battalion to get through. A hundred or so prisoners fell into our hands, but the occupied trench, battered on its flanks by enemy fire, had to be abandoned. The operation had failed except for its partial success on that point.

My battalion was in reserve and I was able to watch the operation conducted by the 2nd Battalion. It attacked much farther to the right, beneath the big rocks of Casara Zebio Pastorile[11]. This was a change in plan imposed by the division commander, who thought the artillery should not be used at that point but that another surprise attack should be launched. In any event, two batteries were not enough to cover the front of an entire division, so they were forced to do without it. The general had not lost his faith in the Farina cuirasses. His idea was that an armored company, advancing in compact formation, would constitute an avalanche of steel, against which all the enemy's firepower would be impotent. Lieutenant Colonel Carriera had been the only one to show any enthusiasm for the plan, and his battalion had been called upon to execute it.

I was in the trench, a spectator, next to the command of the 2nd Battalion. The 6th Company, commanded by Lieutenant Fiorelli, was wearing the cuirasses. It was supposed to lead the way, with the other companies to follow. The lieutenant, he too wearing the armor, was the first to leave our trench, and his company was right behind him. The operation didn't last more than a few minutes. The enemy machine guns, from on top of the crags, opened fire on the company immediately and destroyed it. They had managed to take no more than a few steps beyond our trenches. The soldiers' bodies were lying there in front of us with their armor ripped open, as though they had been hit by the light mountain guns. The lieutenant colonel had to suspend the operation.

The distance from our trenches to the crags, at the point where the 6th Company had launched the attack, was no less than two hundred meters. Taking advantage of the bushes, we tried to carry the wounded back in. While the lieutenant colonel was looking at the first casualties to arrive back in the trench, he remained exposed and was wounded in the arm. He cried out and fell to the ground, unconscious.

The wound didn't look serious, but the bullet had gone through his arm from side to side. He was tall and husky, but stretched out on the ground like that, he blocked the whole trench and looked immensely taller and huskier. His face had turned into a pasty white mask and for a minute it was thought he had expired. His men gathered around him and brought him back to consciousness with splashes of water. He was breathing with violent gasps and gnashing his teeth. He managed to say a few words but he didn't open his eyes. His adjutant, the Greek professor, held a canteen of brandy up to his mouth and he gulped it all down. I wasn't standing very close to him, but I could hear it gurgling in his throat so noisily it sounded to me like water whirling down the sides of a funnel.

The wounded were still being carried back to the trench. The lieutenant colonel, supported by two soldiers, his back leaning against the parapet, managed to sit up. An orderly was bandaging his arm. Without opening his eyes, he asked in the voice of a little boy, "What time is it?"

"Ten o'clock," the adjutant said.

"What time was it when I got wounded?"

"It was maybe a quarter to ten."

The captain of the 5th Company, the senior officer in the battalion, asked if he should take command.

"No," the lieutenant colonel replied, "the battalion is still under my command."

He asked about the progress of the operation and gave a few orders.

Lieutenant Fiorelli was also carried back to the line. His armor was ripped open at the shoulder; you could have put your hand through the hole. After a long struggle to free himself from all that useless steel, he was ready to be bandaged. His collarbone and the bone in his upper arm were fractured.

Every now and again the lieutenant colonel asked what time it was. When it was a quarter past ten, he asked his adjutant to come closer to him and, his eyes still closed, dictated to him the following proposal, which went more or less like this:

From: Command, 2nd Battalion, 399th Infantry
To: Command, 399th Infantry
The undersigned, Lieutenant Colonel Cavalier Michele Carriera, commander of the 2nd Battalion,

399th Infantry, is honored to bring to the attention of the regiment command the conduct of Lieutenant Colonel Cavalier Michele Carriera during the battle of August 17, 1916. Gravely wounded in the arm as he was leading his battalion in an assault on the enemy, despite the serious loss of blood and great pain and suffering, he refused to relinquish command of his battalion and have himself transported for medical treatment. With heroic resolve, heedless of the danger, he chose to remain in the midst of his men and to keep directing the attack, taking all necessary measures. Only after half an hour, having ascertained the good progress of the operation and given his successor the order to carry on, did he give up his command and leave the battalion.

For this steadfast demeanor, contemplated by the Royal Decree of 1848, the undersigned is honored to propose to this command the name of Lieutenant Colonel Cavalier Michele Carriera for the Silver Medal for Military Valor. Admirable example to his subordinates of bravery and self-sacrifice, et cetera, et cetera.

Lieutenant Colonel in S.A.P.
Commander, 2nd Battalion

Only then did he open his eyes. He took out his pen and signed "Michele Carriera." And closed his eyes again.

The captain of the 5th assumed command of the battalion and the orderlies carried off the lieutenant colonel on a stretcher. The Greek professor had remained standing, holding the pen and paper, he, too, amazed. After thinking for a minute or so he scrupulously noted, "I forgot to put the date." He added "Casara Zebio, August 17, 1916."

As these extraordinary bureaucratic operations were being carried out, the trench was filling up with wounded. The Austrians were still firing up and down the entire line because the battle was still raging in the sector. The lieutenant colonel had just left when the medical cadet from my battalion arrived in the trench, sent by his medical lieutenant to dress his first wounds. A medical student at the University of Naples, he wasn't a doctor yet. The uproar of war left him bewildered. He saw an abandoned cuirass sitting on the parapet and, not knowing about the failed experiment with the cuirasses, tried to put it on. Somebody pointed out to him the others, still wrapped around the wounded, which were riddled with holes as though they were cotton T-shirts. From that moment, having forgotten his mission, he lost his head completely. The trench wall was high, higher than he was tall, but he walked bent over, his eyes lost, tripping over the wounded.

"Attend to the wounded and treat them!" an irate lieutenant from the battalion command yelled at him.

The cadet looked at him with a desperate smile. Incapable of standing up, he let himself drop to the ground and crawled on his hands and feet.

"Alarm!" came a shout from the far right flank of our trench. "Alarm! Alarm!"

It was all a confused and chaotic running around. The battalion pressed against the loopholes, and our machine guns, which up to then hadn't been shooting, opened fire. I went over to a loophole as well and saw an Austrian column that, having come down on the far side of the rocks at the edge of the ravine, was attacking the far left flank of our trench. Stopped by the sudden burst of machine-gun fire, they took cover behind the rocks. When calm returned and we looked for the medical cadet, we realized he had disappeared.

Half an hour later, returning to my battalion, I passed by the first aid station, where Lieutenant Fiorelli had been transported. We had met back in Padova, where he was an engineering student, and I wanted to get a better idea of how serious his wound was. As I was walking through the passageway, I heard the joyous voice of song, accompanied by a mandolin, coming from a lateral dugout. I was baffled. Who could be singing so cheerfully on the day of an attack, surrounded by the dead and wounded? I knew that dugout was used as a storage area for the pharmacy. I went over to it and raised the curtain that closed the entrance. The entryway was lit up by candlelight coming from the back room. Next to the candle, sitting on a box of medicine, was the medical cadet. It was he, all by himself, who was singing a Neapolitan tune and playing the mandolin.[12] Two bottles of Mandarinetto liqueur were sitting beside him: one empty, the other half-full.

A mare chiare ce sta 'na finestra
A mare chiare . . .
A mare chiare . . .

I went in. His eyes wide open, the cadet stopped his singing and let the mandolin drop from his hands. He looked at me amazed, as though he had seen a ghost.

Between lieutenants and cadets we used the informal "tu." But in order to highlight even more my disgust and the difference in rank between us, I laid into him using the formal "lei."

"You, Signor Cadet, should be ashamed of yourself! Is this your post?"

At attention, but bent over because his head was touching the vaulted ceiling of the dugout, he didn't answer me.

"Was it you," I yelled, "who drank these bottles?"

With a thin reed of a voice and the expression of a supplicant, he replied, "Excellency, yes."

XVIII

In the days of calm that followed, word spread through the brigade that we were finally going to be given a rest. Among ourselves, that was all we could talk about. The division commander was informed of this and responded with a daily order that ended with, "Let it be known to everyone, officers and soldiers alike: Short of victory, the only rest is death." There was no more talk of rest.

The event had no repercussions in the history of the war, but to allow for a better understanding of these notes, I must inform the reader that I was promoted to lieutenant in command of a company. Lieutenants with a red stripe, they were called back then. I took over command of the 10th Company, in which I had served since the beginning of the war and which I had commanded on the Carso.

On the same day, almost as though they were celebrating my advancement, the Austrians installed a trench cannon and fired several volleys against the trench occupied by my company. From one of its shells that we picked up unexploded, we concluded it was a 37mm. The piece never fired more than a few consecutive rounds, now on one loophole, now on another, and two of our lookouts were wounded. Despite our efforts to locate it, we weren't able to figure out if it had been set up in a trench or behind the lines.

Each day at a different time, with unprovoked volleys, the little cannon pelted our line. The division commander heard the shots and asked for an explanation. The brigade command gave him all the information it had received. The general was not satisfied and came up to the trench.

At that time I was on the line. My company occupied the right side of the battalion's sector and extended out as far as a few meters short of loophole 14, which was at the line's highest elevation. Further to the right, and immediately after us, connected to my company, was the machine-gun section, with two weapons, commanded by Lieutenant Ottolenghi. He was responsible for the sector's right flank.

General Leone came directly into the trench without stopping at the battalion command. I saw him arrive and went to greet him.

He immediately asked me for news about the little cannon. I told him what I knew. When my exposition was over, he peppered me with questions, and I admired yet again his interest in the details and his desire for mathematical control. He insisted on checking, one by one, about fifty loopholes and remained in my company's sector for at least an hour.

"Your loopholes," he said to me finally, "look down at the ground like the traps in the Palazzo della Signoria, and they look more like they were made for hunting crickets than for observing the enemy trenches."

I was careful not to smile, he spoke in such a somber tone. Nevertheless, I explained to him the reasons why, in my sector, the loopholes couldn't have been made any other way, because of the lay of the terrain and the position of the trees and rocks in front of the trench.

"It's not the fault of the builders but of the nature of the terrain. Take a look at this loophole here, general. If we move its range of fire more to the left, we end up running into that fir tree out there, and we can't see anything anymore. If we move it right, we're blocked by that rock. Nor can we raise it any higher, because those bushes there would block our vision."

"You're right," he told me in the end. "We can't make the loopholes the way we'd like them to be. But how am I supposed to figure out the position of that annoying little cannon? I want to silence it once and for all with my artillery."

The general had turned reasonable and moderate. When we came to the last loophole in my sector he even became courteous.

"I saw you for the first time on Mount Fior, I think."

"Yes, sir, general."

"You can call yourself lucky. You still haven't been killed."

"No, sir, general."

To my great surprise, he pulled out a cigarette case and offered me one. But he didn't light his and I didn't dare light mine.

We had arrived at the far end of my company. I said, "This is where my sector ends, and the machine-gun sector begins. Would you like me to accompany you farther?"

"Yes, accompany me. Thank you. Be so kind as to accompany me."

He couldn't have been more courteous. I was enchanted with him. Had he undergone some kind of character change?

We were already in the machine-gun sector and I was walking in front of the general. Having most likely been informed, Lieutenant Ottolenghi came to meet us. I pointed him out to the general and said, "Here is the lieutenant in command of this sector."

I let him pass and the general found himself facing Lieutenant Ottolenghi. The lieutenant introduced himself.

"Show me your loopholes," said the general. "Do you know your loopholes? Have you been in this sector for a long time?"

"For over a week, general. I've had all the loopholes repositioned myself. I know them well."

Ottolenghi led the way, and the general followed. I was behind him, and behind me were the two carabinieri with whom the general had come up to the line, and my orderly. The trenches were calm. During that entire inspection, the little cannon hadn't made itself heard. There was nothing coming from the enemy line except, every now and again, a rifle shot, which got a response from our lookouts.

Ottolenghi stopped between two loopholes, which he defined as secondary, and said, "These are loopholes made for shooting at the foot of our entanglements, not for observation."

The general took a long look, first at one and then at the other.

"These loopholes can't be used for observation or for

shooting," he concluded. "You will do me the favor or ordering them to be destroyed. Have two new ones built. Where are your main loopholes?"

The general had become authoritarian again.

"Up ahead here we have the best loophole in the whole sector," replied Ottolenghi. "You can see all the terrain in front of it and up and down the whole enemy line, every part of it. I don't think a better loophole exists. It's right here. Loophole fourteen."

Loophole 14, I said to myself. Since I hadn't seen that sector for several days, I deduced that Ottolenghi must have eliminated some loopholes, shifted the numbers, and attributed number 14 to another loophole.

At the first curve in the trench, Ottolenghi stopped. There had been no changes made in the trench. The loopholes were all the same. Detached from the others, beyond the curve, higher than the others and easily distinguishable, was loophole 14 with its steel plate. Ottolenghi had stopped beyond the loophole, leaving it between him and the general.

"Look here," said the general, raising the shutter and immediately letting it drop. "The hole is small and doesn't allow observation by more than one person."

I made some noise, banging my walking stick against some stones, trying to get Ottolenghi's attention. I looked for his eyes in order to make a sign that he should desist. He didn't look at me. He certainly understood, but didn't want to look at me. His face had turned white. My heart was trembling.

Instinctively, I opened my mouth to call out to the general.

But I didn't speak. I don't want to pretend that I had no responsibility for what might have happened then. A general was about to be killed. I was present, I could have prevented it, and I didn't say a word.

The general walked over in front of the loophole. He moved in behind the shield, bent his head down until it touched the steel, raised the shutter, and put his eye up to the hole. I closed my eyes.

How long that wait lasted I couldn't say. I kept my eyes closed the whole time. I didn't hear any shots.

The general said, "It's magnificent! Magnificent!"

I opened my eyes and saw the general still at the loophole. Without moving, he started talking, "Here, now, it looks to me like . . . the little cannon is positioned in the trench, but it seems unlikely . . . Maybe yes . . . where the trench is in a staggered line, it's possible . . . But I don't think so . . . You can see so well from here . . . Bravo, lieutenant! . . . It's likely that it's positioned behind the trench, a few meters behind . . . in the trees . . ."

Ottolenghi suggested, "Look closely, general, to the left, where there's a white sack. You see it?"

"Yes, I see it, it's very clear. Everything is very clear."

"I have the impression that the little cannon is there. You don't notice anything, can't see any smoke, but that's where the noise comes from. Can you see that?"

"Yes, I see."

"Look carefully, don't move."

"It's likely . . . it's likely . . ."

"With your permission, now, I'll have our line come to

life. I'll have a machine gun open fire. That should provoke the little cannon into shooting back, for reprisal."

"Yes, lieutenant, have them start shooting."

The general stepped back from the loophole and let the shutter fall. Ottolenghi gave the order to a machine gun to fire. A second later it opened fire. The general went back to the loophole and raised the shutter again.

The little cannon was silent. The only response from the enemy trench was a few rifle shots. Two or three times, the general pulled his face away from the loophole to say something to Ottolenghi, and the sunlight burst in through the hole. As the machine gun kept on firing, the general looked out first with his left eye then with his right.

The noise of the isolated shots and the machine-gun fire failed to rouse the Austrian sharpshooter manning the tripod rifle.

The general moved away from the loophole. Ottolenghi was vexed.

"I'll order the artillery to fire some volleys," he proposed to the general. "You'd do well to keep looking a little longer."

"No," replied the general, "enough for now. Bravo, lieutenant! Tomorrow I'll have my chief of general staff come here, so he can get a better idea of the enemy positions. Good-bye."

He shook both of our hands and walked off, followed by his two carabinieri. We were left alone.

"You must be crazy!" I exclaimed.

My orderly was only a few steps away. It didn't appear that he was looking or listening.

Ottolenghi didn't even answer me. He was red in the face and walking around in circles.

"You want to bet that if I open the loophole that imbecile sharpshooter will wake up?"

He took a coin out of his pocket, grasped its edge lightly between his thumb and index finger, raised the shutter, and held the coin up to the hole. A strip of sunlight lit up the hole. And what came next was all one: the hissing of the bullet and the crack of the rifle shot. The coin, shot out of his hand, flew off into the fir trees.

Ottolenghi seemed to have lost all self-control. Furious, he stamped his feet on the ground, bit his fingers, and cursed.

"And now he wants to send us his chief of staff!"

That night we dismantled loophole 14.

XIX

There was no more talk of new assaults. Calm seemed to have settled in over the valley for a good long time. On one side and the other, positions were reinforced. The pioneers worked through the night. The little 37mm cannon continued to pester us, still invisible. Whole days went by without it firing a shot, then, out of the blue, it would open fire on a loophole and wound one of our lookouts.

My battalion was still on the line and we were waiting for the relief battalion to replace us. I wanted to be able to give precise instructions to the commander of the unit that would be taking our place. Day and night, I had a special observation detail on duty, in the hope that the flash of the cannon shot or the movements of its crew might give away its position.

The night before the change of battalions, since the observation details hadn't produced any results, I decided to go on observation myself, accompanied by a corporal. The corporal had gone out frequently on patrol and had a good feel for the terrain. The moonlight was shining through the trees and, whenever the occasional rocket whizzed by, the sudden flash of light made it look like the forest was moving. You couldn't always tell if it was an illusion. It might well have been men moving around out there and not just trees that, because of the speed of the light from the rockets passing through their limbs, looked like they were moving. The two of us had gone out from the far left end of our company, at the point where our trenches were closest to the enemy trenches. Moving on all fours, we took cover behind a bush, about ten meters beyond our line and thirty or so meters from the Austrian line. There was a slight depression between our trenches and the bush, and it crowned a rise in the terrain dominating the trench in front of it.

We were stuck there, immobile, unable to decide whether to advance farther or stay put, when there seemed to be some movement in the enemy trenches, off to our left. There were no trees in front of that part of the trench so what we were seeing couldn't have been an optical illusion. Anyway, we realized that we were in a spot from where we could see into the enemy trench, right down the line. We couldn't do that from any other point. I decided to stay there all night so we would be able to observe the enemy trench coming to life at the first light of dawn. Whether the little cannon fired or not didn't matter anymore. What was essential was maintaining that unhoped-for observation point.

The bush and the rising terrain masked our presence and protected us so well that I decided to connect them directly to our line and make them into a permanent, hidden observation point. I sent the corporal back and had him bring back a sergeant in the pioneers, whom I instructed on how to do the work. In just a few hours, a communications passage had been dug between our trench and the bush. The noise of the work was covered by the noise of the shots going off up and down our line. The passageway wasn't deep, but it was possible for a man to crawl through it, and stay covered, even during the day. The dirt from the digging was carried back into the trench, and there were no visible signs of the excavation. Small, freshly cut tree branches and bushes completed the disguise.

Hunched behind the bush, the corporal and I lay in wait all through the night without managing to make out any signs of life in the enemy trench. But dawn made our wait worthwhile. First came the vague movement of some shadows in the passageways, then, inside the trench, some soldiers appeared carrying pots. This had to be the coffee detail. The soldiers passed by, one or two at a time, without bending their heads, sure as they were that they couldn't be seen, that the trenches and the lateral crossways protected them from observation and from possible raking gunfire from our line. I'd never seen anything like it before. The Austrians were right there, up close, almost at arm's length, calm and unawares, like so many passersby on a city sidewalk. A strange feeling came over me. Not wanting to talk, I squeezed the arm of the corporal, who was on my right, to communicate my amazement to him. He, too, was intent and surprised, and I could feel the trembling that came over him from holding his breath for so long. An unknown life was suddenly showing itself to our eyes. Those indomitable trenches, against which we had launched so many futile attacks, had nevertheless ended up seeming inanimate, like dismal empty structures, uninhabited by living beings, a refuge for mysterious and terrible ghosts. Now they were showing themselves to us, in their actual lived life. The enemy, the enemy, the Austrians, the Austrians! . . . There is the enemy and there are the Austrians. Men and soldiers like us, made like us, in uniform like us, who were now moving, talking, making themselves coffee, exactly as, at the same time, our comrades were doing behind us. Strange. Nothing like that had ever crossed my mind. Now they were making themselves coffee. Bizarre! So why shouldn't they be making themselves coffee? Why in the world did it seem so extraordinary to me that they should make themselves coffee? And, around ten or eleven, they would have their rations, exactly like us. Did I think perhaps that the enemy could live without drinking and eating? Of course not. So what was the reason for my surprise?

They were so close to us that we could count them, one by one. In the trench, between two crossways, there was a little round space where somebody, every now and again, stopped for a minute. You could tell they were talking, but the sound of their voices didn't reach us. That space must have been in front of a shelter that was bigger than the others, because there was more movement around it. The movement stopped when an officer arrived. You could tell he was an officer from the way he was dressed. He had shoes and gaiters made of yellow leather and his uniform looked brand new. Probably he had just arrived a few days ago, maybe fresh out of a military academy. He was very young and his blond hair made him look even younger. He couldn't have been any more than seventeen.

Upon his arrival, the soldiers all scattered and there was nobody left in the round space but him. The coffee distribution was about to begin. All I could see was the officer.

I had been in the war since it began. Fighting in a war for years means acquiring the habits and the mind-set of war. This big-game hunting of men by men was not much different from the other big-game hunting. I did not see a man there. All I saw was the enemy. After so much waiting, so many patrols, so much lost sleep, he was coming out into the open. The hunt had gone well. Mechanically, without a thought, without any conscious intent to do so, but just like that, just from instinct, I grabbed the corporal's rifle. He gave it up to me and I took it. If we had been on the ground, as on the other nights, flat on our bellies behind the bush, I probably would have fired immediately, without wasting a second. But I was on my knees in the newly dug ditch, and the bush was in front of me like a shield in a shooting gallery. It was as though I were on a shooting range and I had all the time I wanted to take aim. I planted my elbows firmly on the ground and started to aim.

The Austrian officer lit a cigarette. Now he was smoking. That cigarette suddenly created a relationship between us. As soon as I saw his puff of smoke I felt the need to smoke. That desire of mine reminded me that I had some cigarettes too. In an instant, my act of taking aim, which had been automatic, became deliberate. I became aware that I was aiming, and that I was aiming at someone. My index finger, pressing on the trigger, eased off. I was thinking. I had been forced to think.

Sure, I was consciously fighting in the war and I justified

that morally and politically. My conscience as a man and as a citizen was not in conflict with my duty as a soldier. The war, for me, was a dire necessity, terrible surely, but one whose demands I obeyed, as one of life's many thankless but inevitable necessities. So I was fighting in the war and I had soldiers under my command. Morally, then, I was fighting twice. I had already taken part in a lot of battles. That I should shoot at an enemy officer was, therefore, in the logic of things. Even more than that, I demanded of my soldiers that they stay alert on their watch and that they shoot accurately if the enemy came into their sights. Why wouldn't I, now, shoot at that officer? It was my duty to shoot. I felt it was my duty. If I didn't feel it was my duty, it would be monstrous for me to continue fighting in the war and to make others do so as well. No, there was no doubt; it was my duty to shoot.

And yet I wasn't shooting. My thoughts worked themselves out calmly. I wasn't at all nervous. The previous night, before leaving the trench, I had slept four or five hours; I felt fine. Behind that bush, down in the ditch, I was not threatened by any danger. I couldn't have been more relaxed in a room in my own house, in my hometown.

Maybe it was that complete calm that drove off my war-fighting spirit. In front of me was an officer, young, unconscious of the looming danger. I couldn't miss. I could have taken a thousand shots at that distance without missing even one. All I had to do was pull the trigger and he would collapse to the ground. This certainty that his life depended on my will made me hesitant. I had a man in front of me. A man!

A man!

I could make out his eyes and the features of his face. The early morning light was getting brighter and the sun was peeking out from behind the mountaintops. To shoot like this, from a few steps away, at a man . . . like shooting a wild boar!

I started thinking that maybe I wasn't going to shoot. I thought: Leading a hundred men, or a thousand, in an assault against another hundred, or another thousand, is one thing. Taking a man, separating him from the rest of the men, and then saying, "There, stand still, I'm going to shoot you, I'm going to kill you," is another. It's a totally different thing. Fighting a war is one thing, killing a man is something else. To kill a man, like that, is to murder a man.

I'm not sure up until what point my thoughts proceeded logically. What's certain is that I had lowered the rifle and I wasn't shooting. Within me two consciousnesses had formed, two individualities, one hostile to the other. I said to myself, "Hey! You're not going to be the one to kill a man like this!"

Even I, who lived through those moments, would not be able now to give an accurate description of that psychological process. There's a jump there that, today, I can't see clearly anymore. And I still ask myself how, having reached that conclusion, I could have thought to have someone else do what I myself didn't feel I could do in good conscience. I had the rifle on the ground, sticking under the bush. The corporal was pressing up against my side. I handed him the butt of the rifle and said to him, barely whispering, "You know . . . like this . . . one man alone . . . I can't shoot. You, do you want to?"

The corporal took the rifle butt in hand and responded, "Me neither."

We made our way back to the trench on all fours. The coffee had already been distributed and we poured some for ourselves, too.

That night, just after sundown, the relief battalion replaced us.

XX

It looked as though our operations, on orders from above, had come to a halt. They were proceeding on other fronts, mainly on the Carso. The high plateau was immersed in calm again. In mid-September, the brigade was sent to rest, near Foza, for fifteen days. We were finally issued clothes and underwear and we cleaned ourselves up like new. For all of us those fifteen days went by like fifteen nights. All we did was sleep.

In October, with winter coming on—in the mountains it arrives in the autumn—our shifts in the trenches, gloomy and monotonous, started up again. Despite it all, they were no worse than the normal, everyday lives led my millions of miners in the great mineral basins of Europe. There were some casualties, but rarely was anyone killed. Occasionally, the explosion of a big-caliber gun or a spigot mortar provoked a catastrophe, like the explosion of firedamp in a well. And life always returned to normal. Trench, rest, another kilometer, trench. Cold, snow, ice, avalanches don't make war any harder for healthy men. They are elements that are well known to anyone who lives in the mountains or in snowy regions. War, for the infantry, is the assault. Without the assault, what you have is hard work, not war.

That's why, of all those long winter months, each the same as the one before, not only is my memory vague, I have no memory at all. Like my childhood years spent in a boarding school. I must, therefore, skip over entire months, pausing on just a few episodes, some of which lasted only minutes, that I lived intensely, and that are still deep in my memory.

General Leone, promoted to a higher command, left our division. We celebrated for a week. His successor, General Piccolomini, arrived when the brigade was on the line. He preferred not to wait to visit the trenches and introduce himself to his troops.

My company was on the line, in the same sector on the right. An orderly from the battalion command warned me he was coming, and I went to meet him. General Leone was ghostly and stiff, the new general was cheerful and skittish. In my quick comparison I made of the two, General Piccolomini seemed like the best of men.

Where he had been before, I can't recall. He had probably been the head of some military school, because he had a pedagogical cast of mind, heavy on theory. I was expecting questions about my men, about the veterans, about morale in the units, about the trenches, the enemy. With the demeanor of a professor giving an oral exam, he said to me, "Now, let's see, lieutenant. Let's hear how you would define victory. I mean to say our victory, military victory."

That was a question I hadn't anticipated. I put on an

intelligent smile, the kind of smile put on by those who haven't understood a thing but believe it inopportune to say. "I don't understand. Be good enough to explain yourself." By smiling, they try to make their interlocutor understand that they've understood, but in such a discreet way that it's as though they haven't.

The general repeated, "Victory. Have I made myself clear or not? Are we fighting to win or to lose? Obviously, to win."

"Naturally."

"Well, the action of winning is victory. I would like you to define this victory for me."

Now I understood, all too well. And I recalled—I won't say with nostalgia, but with slightly less terror—General Leone, who hadn't made many appearances on the line lately and seemed to have come to his senses.

The general insisted; I had to make a decision and respond.

"I wouldn't know, general. The jurist Paulus affirms . . . affirms . . . that all definitions are dangerous." And, without any sense of pride, on the contrary with a certain timidity, I dared to support my citation with a phrase in Latin, one of the very few that I still remembered from my legal studies.

Faced with a Latin phrase, the general was a bit puzzled. He wasn't expecting it. He had surprised me with victory, but I had surprised him with Paulus. To regain the upper hand, he spoke decisively.

"I am not a priest and I have never been in the seminary. So I don't know Latin."

It seemed prudent to remain silent.

"Let's forget about Paulus. And victory? Victory?" the general asked again.

He noted, with satisfaction, that I was unable to make a pronouncement on the subject and wished to come to my aid himself. He defined victory with words, probably taken from some military manual, that now I can't recall, and that had something to do with a "fit of temper." The general distinguished victory on the offensive from victory on the defensive. In the former, the "fit of temper" was unleashed in time, and in the latter, it was thwarted in time.

I started thinking: Let's hope that, in practice, he's better than General Leone.

The general pulled me out of my reflections. "I bet there's not a single officer in your entire battalion who knows this essential definition."

I thought: I sure hope so. But I said, "Very likely, general."

As we walked the trench there wasn't a sound to be heard except the occasional rifle shot. The general was striding fast and sure and I was just ahead of him. It was clear that he had none of those concerns for his personal safety that are common to those who aren't used to life in the trenches. But his thoughts must still have been fixed on the theory of war. Every time we stopped, he would say to me, "Yes, yes, this is a warrior brigade, but there's not enough thinking. To be ignorant of the most elementary notions! An officer!"

I didn't respond.

"Be careful, general, keep your head down. They shoot in this area."

"So let them shoot!" he replied with contempt.

He moved ahead, bending his head just slightly, not nearly enough. A rifle shot put us on notice that we had to be more prudent. He stopped and said, "I want to give those people an answer of my own."

He stopped a soldier who was walking by with a detail and had him hand over his rifle. He took a few steps forward and stopped at the nearest loophole. It wasn't one of the best. It had been built to guard a stretch of our barbed wire that the undulating terrain made into a favorable spot for unseen incursions by enemy patrols. The loophole overlooked a stretch of land that was quite a distance from the enemy trenches; there was no way anyone could shoot at them from there. It belonged to that category of loophole that General Leone had dubbed suitable for hunting crickets.

The general took a long look, flipped over the rifle's rear sight, and skillfully took aim. Calmly, he fired off, one after another, the six rounds in the cartridge. The soldiers in the detail stopped and looked at him respectfully. The general turned to them.

"I wanted to teach those rascals a lesson personally. Be sure to tell your comrades that your general is not afraid to shoulder a rifle just like one of his soldiers."

He was satisfied and also a little moved. The soldiers knew full well that the loophole did not face the enemy trenches. I didn't believe it was necessary to point out to them that he had shot into the ground beneath our own barbed wire.

I thought the little show was over, when the general

appeared to focus his attention on the barrel of the rifle he had fired. He noticed that it did not have the bayonet inserted, as was required for soldiers in the trenches.

"Where's the bayonet?" he asked me.

I explained to him that the soldiers assigned to a detail never carried their weapons with the bayonet inserted, and that the rifle he was holding belonged to a soldier on a detail.

He asked for the bayonet. The soldier handed it to him immediately. The general grabbed it and looked attentively at the point. The bayonet was well sharpened but there was some rust on the point. I thought: That slacker of a sergeant forgot to inspect the bayonets; now we're in for it. I expected the general to reprimand me, as company commander, and I tried to think of a plausible justification. But he wasn't concerned with me. After carefully examining the point, he asked the soldier, "What's this right here?"

The soldier noticed, too, that the bayonet was dirty and turned red in the face.

The general spoke again. "What's this right here? Don't be embarrassed. Come closer. Look carefully. What's written here? There's something written here."

The soldier went over to him and looked carefully. Not all the soldiers in the company knew how to read. On the contrary, there was a high percentage of illiterate farm boys. I thought to myself: Let's hope he at least knows how to read.

The soldier gave the impression that he did because he had an intelligent-looking face. After examining the bayonet, from the point to the cross, he responded hesitantly, "I don't see a thing, general."

I looked at it carefully, too, but didn't see anything. There wasn't a single letter, either on the blade or on the point. Just rust.

The general pounded the soldier on the back and exclaimed, "Blessed young lad! There's a word written here that everybody can read, even the illiterate, that everyone can see, even the blind, it's so shiny and bright."

The general turned to me and asked me, "Isn't that right, lieutenant?"

Since I hadn't seen a thing either, I couldn't say I had seen something. A little embarrassed myself, I moved my head up, down, and sideways in a kind of half-nod, as if to say: Whatever you say.

Now the general addressed himself to the entire detail, standing at attention with their backs against the parapet. He looked like a tribune.

"What is written is . . . victory. Victory! Yes, victory. Do you understand? It is for victory that we are fighting from the Alps to the sea, from the Adriatic to the Tyrrhenian, from the Tyrrhenian to . . . Victory! Victory in the name of the king . . . in the name of His Majesty the King. Victory in the name of . . ."

The general coughed lightly.

"In the name . . ."

Since the third invocation wouldn't come out, he coughed a second time, and a third. Then, suddenly inspired, he concluded, "Long live the king!"

In the heat of his speech, the general had raised his voice. The Austrians must have heard him. The 37mm cannon, still invisible, fired three shots on the trench. For us there was no danger because we were all safe. In the position we were occupying, the cannon was totally harmless. We didn't even have lookouts posted in that point. The general, who couldn't have known, as we did, how safe we were, remained immobile, as calm as could be. Without losing his composure, he said, "Does it shoot often?"

"Rarely," I replied, "and in reprisal."

"Perhaps they wanted to respond to my rifle shots."

"That's possible."

The general gave back the rifle and the bayonet. The detail went on its way. We were left alone. He looked around warily and resumed our conversation in a very low voice.

"Do all of your men have knives?"

"Not all of them, general. Some do, some don't."

"The bayonet is not enough. In man-to-man combat, especially at night, you have to have a knife. A sharp knife, very sharp, very, very . . . you get what I'm saying?"

"Yes, sir, general."

"How many knives are there in your company?"

I didn't have the slightest idea. Generally speaking, every soldier had a knife or a penknife of his own. There were also some who didn't have one. Experience had taught me that, when confronted with a question like that in the line of duty, it's best to respond with numbers. I made a quick count. At that time there were about two hundred soldiers in my company.

"A hundred and fifty knives," I responded.

"Fixed handles?"

"No, general, I haven't seen a single knife with a fixed handle."

"You don't inspect the knives very often, do you?"

"No, general. Since the knives are the soldiers' personal property, It doesn't seem necessary."

"From now on, do it."

"Yes, sir."

"Do your soldiers use them often?"

"Yes, sir."

The general lowered his voice again and, moving in closer, asked me, almost whispering in my ear, "For what purpose?"

In the same tone of voice I answered, "To cut bread . . ."

The general opened his eyes wide, wide, wide. I couldn't take it back.

". . . meat . . . cheese . . ."

The general was devouring me with his eyes. I went on.

". . . to peel oranges. . ."

"No, no," the general said, a horrified look on his face. "No, I mean in combat."

I concentrated for a second, the low tone of our voices being favorable to meditation. In combat? I didn't want to jeopardize the outcome of that inspection, which, despite all the hitches, promised to turn out well. But how could I answer that? In combat! We hadn't been able to get close enough to the Austrians to get at them with rifles, let alone knives! Instead of responding, I repeated, almost in a whisper, "In combat?"

The general's thoughts were racing. He didn't notice that I hadn't responded to his question. He went on, "It goes without saying that the rifle with the bayonet inserted has to be held with both hands. To avoid being caught unprepared, you have to stick your knife between your teeth."

And he imitated the gesture, sticking his index finger between his teeth. The strange pose he had adopted and the look on his face that went with it, the hairs of his mustache standing straight up on his upper lip, reminded me of an otter with a fish in its mouth. I nodded slightly to show I understood.

"And the blow has to be fast. To the heart or to the throat, it doesn't matter, as long as it's quick."

I nodded again, lowering my head. It was obvious that, the less I talked, the better things would go.

"It's better if everyone uses the same kind of knife, with a fixed handle, you understand?"

"Yes, sir."

"Talk to your battalion commander about it."

"Yes, sir."

The general shook my hand, with a cabalistic gesture, as though the two of us had concluded some mysterious pact of war.

The next day, he asked the brigade commander to present him the officers of the two regiments. All the company commanders and all the other officers not on duty were called to report. He wanted to meet all of us and took advantage of the occasion to give a lecture out in the open air. The meeting took place in the sector occupied by the brigade's reserve battalion. The division's daily order had announced the topic of the lecture: "Harmony of understanding."

The day was magnificent. The high plateau had never seen a brighter one.

After a few words of greeting for the officers and the brigade, the general moved on to the main topic. The expression "harmony of understanding" recurred frequently: Harmony of understanding between the commander and his subordinates; harmony of understanding between the infantry and the artillery; harmony of understanding between the officers and their men, et cetera, et cetera. The general employed a lot of definitions. He knew them by heart. I heard, yet again, the definition of victory and its associated fit of temper. But the heart of his speech was understanding. The general let himself go and improvised.

"An understanding that is crystal clear, bright as the sunlight, like the sunlight on this radiant day, in which the infinite atoms dance in divine harmony, just as I would like the officers of my division to dance on days when we do battle."

Often, his speech accelerated. The general had no written notes and spoke off the cuff.

"An understanding that needs only a miniscule key to open a big door; a single word to grasp the significance of an order; an intuition to understand, instantly, at first glance, an unknown fact. For example . . ."

The general came to a halt. He had spotted a semicircular dugout, freshly made, camouflaged with branches and twigs, at the top of a hill, about a hundred meters away from us, along one of the sector's lines of defense.

"For example . . . What's that dugout up there? Do you need to have built it in order to know what it is? No, gentleman, that's not necessary. You don't have to ask. You just need to see it. It's self-evident. You can guess what it is. What is it? It's a machine-gun nest."

The general stood there in the expectant pose of a magician who, having just made a pigeon fly out of a rosebush, waits for the astonished gasps, and the applause, of his audience.

The adjutant from the 2nd Battalion, the Greek professor, was too scrupulous to let anything that was inexact pass without comment. His was the brigade's reserve battalion, and he knew the sector well. Exactness above all. He took a step forward and said, "Permission, general?"

"What's on your mind?" the general replied.

"To be exact, general, to be exact, that's not a machine-gun nest."

"What is it, then?"

"A latrine."

It was an ugly moment for us all. The general coughed. Some of us coughed, too. The lecture was over.

XXI

By November the snow was already deep. After every snowfall we had to raise the height of the trench and move the loopholes up above the level of the snow. A new army commander had arrived and there was talk of action in the offing. Day by day the corps of engineers built portable bridges and ladders and we practiced with them. The bridges were made of woven tree branches and were supposed to be used to pass over the enemy entanglements. The ladders, made of wood, twenty to twenty-five feet long, were meant to enable us to scale the trenches facing our right sector, which the Austrians had built on the rocks. Bridges and ladders were the topics of discussion and gags, day and night. An operation seemed imminent.

My company was on the line, at the far end of the right sector, where the distance between our trenches and the Austrians' was greatest. To our right were the big rocky crags, to our left the narrow ravine, almost treeless. On the right and left the two trenches came closer together; in the middle they moved farther apart until there were some three hundred meters between them. In that middle section, the Austrian trenches were on the slope of the mountain and dominated ours, about thirty meters below.

The battalion command had sent me the soldier Giuseppe Marrasi, punished with fifteen days of restriction and assigned to my company. Some time ago, to get away from life in the trench, he had let it be understood that he knew German and had been assigned to a telephone interception station. When it was discovered that he didn't know the language, he was punished and sent back to the battalion. He belonged to the 9th Company and I hadn't seen him again since Mount Fior. I assigned him to the 2nd Platoon, and he reported immediately for duty because in the trenches you didn't have to do jail time and punishment was commuted to docking your pay.

That night, during an inspection on the line, my attention was drawn by a conversation that was taking place in the 2nd Platoon's shelter, about twenty or thirty meters behind the trenches. I walked over there. The men were smoking and chatting in low voices around the woodstoves. The platoon had no officers and the NCO who commanded it, Sergeant Cosello, was the only one not talking. Sitting on the ground with his legs crossed, he was smoking a clay pipe with an unusually long stem. He smoked and listened.

"I was born on Friday," one soldier said, "and it was clear from the start I wasn't going to be lucky. That same day, my mother died. The day I got drafted was a Friday; my first time in combat was a Friday. The first time I got wounded was a

Friday, and it was Friday when I got wounded the second time. It's a sure thing they're going to kill me on a Friday. I'll bet you anything our attack is scheduled for next Friday."

"I was born on Sunday," another guy said, "and I'm no luckier than you. My mother died six months later, which is no big difference. My father had to get married again in order to raise me because, on the money he made, he couldn't afford to pay a nanny. My stepmother beat me like a mattress. That's my first childhood memory. I wouldn't wish my life on a dog. Then came the war. You remember when the grenade exploded between my legs? Who was there?"

"I was there."

"It was a Sunday. I'd be happy to give you my birthday."

"And how about you, when were you born, Marrasi?"

Marrasi didn't respond.

"If there actually is a day of the week that's lucky, then it's when you were born. Tell the truth: How many battles have you fought in? With one excuse or another you've avoided them all. Now that's lucky."

Marrasi defended himself by attacking.

"Who wants to give me half a cigar?" he asked.

"*Ja,* half a cigar?"

"*Ja, ja!*"

"*Kamarad,* half a cigar!"

They were making fun of his German, and nobody gave him the cigar.

"And that shot in the hand? What a clever shot!"

"How did you manage to shoot it?

"But when you were taken prisoner, not much luck there, I wouldn't say! That time you weren't very lucky at all!"

All the men were laughing. The sergeant, impassive, went on smoking his pipe.

I forgot all about Marrasi. The next day I was in my barracks working on the drawings the battalion command had asked me for. It must have been around two in the afternoon. A cry of alarm rang out from the company's part of the trench, followed by a rifle shot. Immediately, the whole line opened fire. Lickety-split I was back in the trench. The soldiers were running to the loopholes. In the middle of the narrow valley, beyond the line of our entanglements, Marrasi, his legs buried in snow, his hands held high over his head, was advancing toward the enemy trenches. Over the din of the rifle shots, you could hear the baritone voice of Sergeant Cosello.

"Shoot the deserter!"

The enemy trench was silent.

I had to run to answer the phone in the trench. The battalion commander was calling to ask me for an explanation of what was going on. His voice was agitated.

"What is it, what is it? Do you want me to send reinforcements?"

I reassured him, "No, no. One of our soldiers is going over to the enemy, alone, unarmed, and the company is firing at him. The Austrians don't want to scare him so they're not shooting."

"What a disgrace for the battalion!"

"I know, I know. You don't have to tell me. What should I do?"

"Send him back to me, alive or dead!"

"Well, alive won't be easy. They're all shooting at him."

"So much the better. Better dead. Send him to me dead."

"All right. Can I go now?"

"Yes, go ahead, and send me news as soon as you can."

I went back to the loophole. The company's fire had been supplemented by the battalion's two machine guns. Marrasi was still moving forward but he was struggling. On the other side of the valley floor, the terrain was steep, and the snow was still very deep. I was amazed that he hadn't fallen down yet, when I noticed that behind him, about fifty meters away, was Sergeant Cosello, he, too, half-buried in the snow. He was holding his rifle with both hands and, after each step, he took a shot at Marrasi. But Marrasi wouldn't go down. Shouting as loud as I could, I ordered the sergeant to come back inside the trench.

The sergeant stopped. He was standing in the middle of the valley. I was afraid the Austrians would start shooting at him and I repeated my order. The Austrians didn't shoot. He turned around and shouted at me, "Yes, sir!"

His legs were buried in the snow. Standing still, he took careful aim and emptied his whole cartridge on the deserter. Marrasi fell face down in the snow. I thought he had been hit. But, a few seconds later, he got up and started walking forward again. The whole line kept on firing at him.

Marrasi kept walking. Even the sergeant, who was a sharpshooter, had missed him. I've always noticed that, in moments of excitement, soldiers look and shoot with their eyes open, without taking aim.

The sergeant came back in. He came to me, dripping with sweat, and he could hardly talk.

"What a disgrace! What a dishonor!" he gasped. "The 2nd Platoon is dishonored."

The 2nd Platoon was dishonored. The company was dishonored. The battalion was dishonored. Pretty soon, the dishonored would include the regiment, the brigade, the division, the army corps and, in all likelihood, the entire army. Marrasi kept moving forward.

The orderly on telephone duty rushed over to tell me that the battalion commander was on the line again, because the regiment commander wanted to be brought up to date.

"Tell him I'm in the trench and I can't get away. I'll come in a few minutes."

The orderly vanished.

Marrasi was getting farther and farther away from us. The Austrians had two barbed-wire entanglements in front of their trenches. He had reached the first. It was almost entirely covered with snow, but the obstacle was every bit as insurmountable. He grabbed on to the wires, shook them, tried to climb over them, but to no avail. He realized he wouldn't be able to get through. Discouraged, he stopped for a minute and held his head in his hands. He looked like he no longer had the strength to go on. He took a few steps around the same point, desperate. He kept on walking in circles, lost, but invulnerable, under fire from our trenches.

Marrasi got a hold of himself. Resolutely, he walked over to a tree just a few meters away. The tree was along the line of the entanglements, on the outside, toward us, and the Austrians had propped a cheval-de-frise up against it, on the other side. Marrasi unlatched his rifle sling, which was still fastened to his belt, with the two cartridge pouches. Nimbly, he climbed up onto the tree trunk. He wasn't stymied anymore. He was already a couple of meters above ground level. He took a big jump and plummeted into the snow on the other side of the barbed wire. He had passed the first barrier.

The orderly on phone duty came to me again. The battalion commander, besieged by requests from the regiment commander, who in turn was under permanent siege by the brigade commander, insistently called me to the phone.

I sent the orderly away, yelling, "Shoot the telephone line and then go to the battalion commander and tell him the line's dead.

"Yes, sir."

"Did you understand me?"

"Yes, sir."

Amid a shower of rifle and machine-gun fire, Marrasi was moving forward again. The last leg of the crossing, the steepest, was also the most challenging. The enemy trench was just a few meters away. A hand came sticking out from a big loophole, waving him on. He started walking toward the loophole. Our sharpshooters, armed with Benaglia rifle grenades, seemed to have him in their sights. He was hit by the explosion from one of the grenades and fell.[13] But he got back up almost immediately. The gunfire from our sector had now become generalized. From the company, it spread to the whole battalion, to the lateral battalions, beyond Mount Interrotto, all the way to Val d'Assa. Everyone was firing; our guys and the Austrians. It sounded like the entire army corps was engaged in combat. Only the trenches on the side of the mountain were still silent.

Marrasi was under the second barbed-wire barrier, no more than two meters from the Austrian trench. There must have been someone at the big loophole speaking to him in Italian, because it seemed to me there was a conversation going on between him and the trench. As he touched the barbed wire, he fell. He was motionless, his legs buried in the snow, his upper body bent over, his arms and hands reaching out. Against this by now inanimate target, the fire from our entire trench raged on unabated.

It took a while before I was able to get our sector to cease firing. And when it ceased, the firing from the sectors to either side continued, and for quite a while. The telephone was dead and I communicated the news to the battalion command in writing. I had to stand firm, until nightfall, against executing the orders of the regiment commander, who kept demanding that I send out a patrol under the command of an officer to bring back the body and wash away the shame of our brigade. In the end the colonel himself came onto the line to verify personally the execution of the order. But that didn't change the situation. The cadaver was still there, three hundred meters from us and only two from the enemy. And it was daytime. The colonel insisted, and I, seeing that every other argument was futile, found a literary refuge. Fresh from my reading of Ariosto, I cited, with complete serenity, the episode of Cloridano and Medoro:

> *Che sarebbe pensier non troppo accorto,*
> *Perder dei vivi per salvar un morto.*
> 'Twould be a thought none too clever,
> To lose the living to save a cadaver.

The colonel answered me, without hesitation, by putting me under arrest. But the patrol didn't go out.

When darkness fell, and we fired our first rocket, we noticed that Marrasi's body had disappeared.

The bridge and ladder operation was postponed.

XXII

With the onset of winter, we began taking turns going on leave. Fifteen days to spend with our families seemed to us like unequaled happiness. Avellini and I were among the most senior officers in the battalion and we should have been among the first to go on leave. But the bridge and ladder operation, postponed several times, was still in the planning stage, and the colonel kept us on in the regiment. Besides, I had to coordinate my leave with my brother, a soldier in an infantry regiment in the Carnia region of Friuli, since we had been granted permission to go home together. But at such a great distance, it was difficult to work out a plan. At Christmas, we were still in the trenches.

Normally, the Austrians respected the religious holidays. On the important feast days there was no shooting from their trenches and their artillery remained quiet, too. But this time, our listening posts had managed to intercept an enemy phonogram concerning a mine that was supposed to be detonated at midnight on Christmas. We believed the mine had been dug out of the rock, under our trenches, on the far right side of our sector. Our listening equipment had picked up the noise of the drills as far back as October, and our command was constantly worried. If we lost our positions in that point, the Austrians, exploiting the surprise, would be able to interrupt not only our lines but also our communications, by occupying the position dominating the valley that connected our two divisions. In addition, the right flank of our brigade would be completely exposed.

Our battalion, better than all the others, knew those positions, and the regiment command ordered two of our companies, the 9th, under Avellini, and mine, the 10th, to stay on the line on Christmas night. That was the night the regiment was scheduled to be relieved, and our two companies were supposed to ensure continuity in that delicate point, where the new arrivals would find themselves unprepared.

After sunset, the regiment moved down to Campomulo to begin its period of rest. The 9th occupied the sector where the mine was, and my company was deployed in support, in the immediate vicinity, to be ready to counterattack after the explosion. Only we officers were informed about what was supposed to happen. The soldiers were only disappointed about having to remain on the line while the rest of the regiment spent Christmas at rest. The distribution of an oversized ration of chocolate and brandy raised some suspicion, but it was swept away by the consideration that the ration was our compensation for taking on the special Christmas duty.

Before moving into position over the mine, Avellini brought me a packet of letters, sealed. The elegance of the packet and the faint smell of perfume it emitted clearly revealed its provenance. I didn't have any exact information, but I knew that Avellini was in love with a young woman. These had to be the letters he had received from her.

With a smile intended to cover up the happy secret, he said to me, "It's nothing very important. On the contrary, it's not related to our duties. But if I get buried by the mine tonight, will you make sure this packet is delivered to the person whose address you'll find in the first sealed envelope?

I didn't want to ask any questions. I didn't want to seem indiscreet. But above all I was afraid that his answer would destroy a hope I had been nurturing amid all my worries and doubts: That the young woman whose letters had been placed in my custody not turn out to be the same one I had been thinking about for a long time now. Avellini and I had been together when we met her, sometime in September, in Marostica, near Bassano. We had been sent to that small town on a mission when the regiment was at rest in Gallio. We were introduced to her and her family by an officer friend, and I was deeply struck by her. I was hoping that I had provoked the same interest on her part. Actually, I felt rather sure that was the case. But Avellini had been able to see her again when she was alone. Since my thoughts so often turned to that house, I was persecuted by the doubt that she preferred Avellini to me. I made up my mind a number of times to talk to him about it, but I never followed through. That night, as Avellini was leaving me with the packet in my hands and heading out to go up to the line, I couldn't resist.

I asked him, "Is she blond?"

He nodded.

"Is she nice looking?"

He answered, half closing his eyes, dreamy, "Beautiful."

I didn't dare ask anything more.

But, I thought, why does it have to be her?

Wasn't it possible he was talking about another woman? Sure, it was possible.

Avellini had good reason to think he was in danger and to make plans in case that night was the last night of his life. But he hadn't taken into account that my life might also be at risk. In war, whoever's in front thinks those behind him are safe. I hadn't really thought about it either, but once I was alone I realized that the packet of letters wasn't all that much safer in my hands than his. After the explosion of the mine, I would have to counterattack, and who knew what I would find. I decided to put the packet in a safe place.

About a hundred meters behind me, blocking the entrance to the valley, was a line formed by two redoubts, with a bunker occupied by a mountain artillery battery. I was good friends with the commander, a captain in the artillery, whom I'd known since he arrived. I had dealt with him repeatedly about numerous things: drawings, topographical reliefs, the construction work on the bunker. On the night in question, I was to have been in continuous contact with him, because the response of his pieces, after the explosion of the mine, was supposed to be coordinated with my company's counterattack. It wasn't long after nightfall. The mine wasn't expected to go off until late, at midnight, according to the intercepted phonogram. I found the captain alone, in the small mess that the battery had built behind its bunker. The officers of a mountain battery in position had the same comforts as the command of an infantry regiment on the front line. The wooden walls were painted and embellished with illustrations of war. The captain was sitting at the still uncleared dinner table. The officers had finished eating and had gone back to their duty stations. The captain had a telephone and two bottles within easy reach: one brandy and one Benedictine. He was drinking and smoking.

"They must be Bosnian Muslims," he said, as soon as he saw me. "Imagine setting off a mine on Christmas night. It's a nice little manger scene they're preparing for us. But I've got my pieces aimed in such a way that, if they really are Mohammedans, tonight they'll be in direct contact with the Prophet."

"I sincerely hope," I said, "that you don't mistake us for Bosnians and start firing into our backs. Remember, not more than a few seconds after the explosion, we'll have already launched our assault and we'll have occupied the positions that you've got your cannons aimed at."

"Come on now, what do you take me for? We're not assault artillery, we can't afford to play games like that. I've arranged for illumination by flares and, from my observation point, I'll be able to make out the smallest details."

Our conversation was centered on mountain artillery as opposed to field artillery, and on the midsize and big-caliber guns that were particularly adept at mistaking their target and firing on our troops. The captain had his men make us some coffee, which was a specialty of his battery. Its special feature was that the coffee was accompanied by three glasses of the finest brandy, which were drunk as follows: one before the coffee, one in the coffee, and one after the coffee. From my previous visits, he knew I didn't drink brandy, and he joked about my being a teetotaling old codger.

I showed him the sealed packet.

"If anything should happen to me tonight, I beg you to deliver this packet to Lieutenant Avellini, from the 9th Company. If he turns out to be no luckier than me, you'll find, in the top envelope inside the packet, the address of the person to whom the packet should be sent."

The captain had already drunk the first part of his brandy-laced coffee.

"Love letters?" he asked me.

I avoided answering and he erupted into uproarious laughter.

"What's there to laugh about?"

"You're right. There's absolutely nothing to laugh about. There's something to cry about."

He was still laughing.

"Do you believe in women?" he asked me.

"Why, don't you?"

"Me? Me? Me?" he repeated in crescendo.

He reached for the bottle of brandy, drank another glass, and said, "There, that's what I believe in."

"That doesn't mean that you can't also believe in women, when necessary."

"I'm thirty-five years old," he said, "and I've been married for six. I've got a little more experience than you do."

"With this particular subject matter experience isn't all that useful."

"Experience teaches you to value life for what it is and not for what you wish it were. Compared to me, you're nothing but a kid. When you've got a woman who's a thousand kilometers away, the only thing to do is forget about her. Don't fool yourself, there's nothing else to do. And for forgetting, there's nothing better than this stuff here."

Then we drank our coffee.

"Because if you don't forget, the only thing left is a pistol shot to the head."

The captain spoke in the most cheerful tone. Certainly the liquor was going to his head, but his words were going to his head, too. He spoke in rapid fire, as if he'd been waiting a long time for the chance to get something off his chest, and he kept saying the same thing over and over. He took a picture out of his wallet.

"Here, take a look. She's beautiful. Beautiful as only a beautiful woman can be. But she's not worth a bottle of brandy."

I took the picture in my hand, but I didn't have time to look at it. He grabbed it away from me violently, jumped to his feet, and threw it into the lighted woodstove.

I was embarrassed and didn't know what to say. He quickly calmed down and took the packet from me.

"Don't worry," he said. "You can count on me."

He changed the subject and started talking about our duties, drinking all the while.

We got up to leave. I was already at the door. He grabbed me by the arm and asked, "You don't think I'm jealous, do you?"

"I wouldn't dream of it!" I replied.

Together, we went to inspect the forward positions. The gun crews were at their pieces, together with their officers. Everything was in order.

I went back to my company. The men were in the shelters, smoking and drinking. I sat down with them and waited for midnight.

At a quarter to, I divided up the men into squads, ready to move out of the shelters and rush to the passageways. As midnight was about to strike, the soldiers realized that some unusual event was about to take place and they questioned each other with their eyes. I told them that we were expecting a surprise attack and that we had to be ready to launch a counterattack. But the closer we got to the appointed hour, the more my thoughts wandered away from my company, from the mine, from all of those places. I kept saying to myself, "It must be her. It can't be anyone but her." And, every time, my doubts fought their way back to the surface and I found all kinds of reasons for comfort. "It's not her. It can't be her." And I saw her again, just as I'd seen her the first time, standing at the window of her home looking out on the street as I was entering the front door of her building, her blond hair falling down onto her forehead, but not enough to hide her bright, smiling eyes.

When I looked at my watch, midnight had already come and gone. The mine hadn't exploded. I sent a messenger to Avellini to ask for news. He responded that he hadn't noticed anything out of the ordinary and that the enemy trenches were on watch just as they were on other nights.

We waited, but not as worried, until dawn. Had our listening posts heard wrong? Had the Austrians played a practical joke on us?

The next morning our two companies were relieved and we joined the regiment at Campomulo. Having retrieved the packet, I gave it back to Avellini.

That same day, the colonel invited us to lunch and informed us that we could go on leave the next day. As we were having our coffee, he asked, "Tell me the truth, sincerely. During this entire war, have you ever lived through anything more dramatic than those few minutes before midnight?"

Avellini hurried to answer. "I made sure I was ready for it, naturally, but my mind was somewhere else."

And he looked at me, smiling, as though I alone could understand him.

XXIII

Avellini and I left together to go on leave. We traveled a good part of the way together as well because his family was in Piedmont and mine was in Sardinia. At the last minute, my brother had had I can't remember what duty-related problem and was forced to delay his departure. I arrived home alone.

My father had aged visibly. I'd always believed he was a strong man, and I realized right away that he had changed. He was depressed and didn't hide his discouragement. My brother and I were his only two children and we were both in the infantry. He harbored no more illusions. He didn't see any hope that both of us would make it back from the war safe and sound. He'd been neglecting his business. Our big old country house, once so full of life, was now nearly empty.

My mother seemed braver than I remembered. I had sent her a lot of letters, mailed from various towns behind the lines, that made her think I was out of danger. But when the wounded soldiers from my regiment came home, they told tales of battles we had fought together, thus destroying, in large part, the illusion I had created. Nevertheless, she seemed full of hope, and she kept my father going, too.

I talked about the war very cautiously. I managed fairly quickly to give them the idea that life on the front line was tolerable and not the nightmare it was made out to be. Our parents had thought that we were constantly involved in furious battles. They had never imagined that we could live for months without fighting and without even seeing the Austrians. They had no idea of the geography of the front, and, even though the maps showed the front to be hundreds of kilometers long, they believed that a battle on one sector necessarily spilled over into or had spectators in the other sectors as well. The way I described it to them, the war didn't sound so unbearable. I also supported my version with the argument that officers don't run the same risks as soldiers and pointed out that my brother was stationed on a peaceful part of the front. But every time my father was alone with me he would give me his unvarnished opinion.

"I'm not going to see the end of this war. And I'm afraid you two aren't going to see it either."

One night we had a relative of ours over for dinner, a foot soldier home on leave after being wounded. We had finished eating and were having coffee. My father asked him, more to keep the conversation going than to solicit his views, "What do you think, Antonio, will the war be over soon?"

Up until that point I had succeeded in steering the conversation away from the war.

Antonio responded with confidence, "It's never going to end. The war is a never-ending slaughter."

My mother didn't understand and asked, "What is it?"

"A never-ending slaughter."

"Even for the officers?"

"For them, too."

When Antonio left, I had no trouble convincing them that he was an alarmist.

I rarely left the house, and my mother's desire to be close to me was so great that she hovered over me all the time. She treated me like a little boy, to the point that at night, when I was going to bed, she offered to help me get undressed and kept coming back to kiss me before retiring to her room. In the morning, it was she, and only she, who brought me my coffee, in bed. And she insisted I have it in bed so she could be with me and talk to me, on and on, about everything.

That time, my leave wasn't very lucky for my parents. I'd been home for just four days when a telegram from the regiment commander called me back up to the front line for urgent and unforeseen necessities. I thought: It's time for the bridge and ladder operation. But I made up the pretense that it was all about purchases of harness and tackle for the horse and mule teams, about which the regiment attributed me greater expertise than I actually had. My father became mute and didn't talk again until it was time for me to go. My mother once again showed herself to be very calm and brave, and that made me feel really good.

My father offered to accompany me on the first leg of the journey. I said good-bye only to my mother, who stayed home. Our farewell was simple. Mamma caressed me and kissed me endlessly, without shedding a tear, even managing to smile. I was amazed by her reassurance. I never would have believed she was so strong. My father, mute again, paced back and forth without looking at us.

We had gone about fifty meters from the house. My father was holding my arm in his. I joked about his ignorance of military regulations and told him he was making me break the rules, because a soldier is not allowed to walk arm in arm, not even with his father. Then I realized that I had forgotten my whip back at the house. I left my father and, striding briskly, retraced our steps.

The front door was still open. I walked in and shouted, "Mamma, I forgot my whip."

In the middle of the living room, next to an overturned chair, Mamma was collapsed on the floor, weeping. I gathered her in my arms and helped her get up. But she couldn't stand up on her own, and in a few seconds she crumbled again. I kept talking to her to try to comfort her, but she just melted into tears. Several minutes must have gone by, because I heard my father's voice shouting impatiently.

"All this time for a whip? You're going to end up missing the train."

I pulled myself away from Mamma and rushed back out.

After traveling for three days with no stops, I reached the high plateau.

Avellini had been called back too, and had arrived before me.

And indeed it was the bridge and ladder operation that was being prepared. The regiment had gone back up to the front line. So I wouldn't lose precious time, the officer in charge of the baggage train gave me a mule and, in just a few hours, I was back in the trench. The artillery was firing throughout the whole sector.

When I got to the front line it was two or three o'clock in the afternoon. My battalion was deployed in the same position as before. A few lookouts were at the loopholes, standing on platforms high above. More snow had fallen in those days and the trench had been raised again to the level of the snow. The lookouts moved around on the platforms like bricklayers building a house. The big logs supporting the overhanging wooden scaffolding made the trench look like a construction site. The rest of the men were distributed along the trench and up and down the passageways, waiting. Because of the constant movement, the snow on the bottom of the trench and passageways had melted and a thick layer of mud had formed, welling up around the soldiers' feet. Their faces had the look of resignation. They were all drinking. The canteens of brandy were in perpetual motion. When I first arrived, I was greeted by a cavernous odor of mud and brandy, and I was reminded of Baudelaire's "*labyrinths fangeux*" in "Le Vin des Chiffonniers."

The sun was nowhere to be seen and it looked like it was getting ready to snow again.

The most senior lieutenant, who commanded the company in my absence, came to meet me and gave me the news. All our men were in the trench, even the ones who were running a fever.

He said to me, "You could have stayed home and finished

your leave in peace. We won't be advancing so much as a meter today. The snow is up to my neck. To make it to the enemy trenches I'd need an elevator."

He was short. But even though I was much taller I wouldn't have been any better off. On that terrain an assault seemed to me like one of the most bizarre things of the war.

I went looking for the battalion commander and found him, like the others, standing in the mud. He was drinking, too. I didn't know him because he had arrived while I was on leave. He was a major, around fifty, who had come from Libya. I was one of the few veterans in the regiment, and he greeted me cordially, as though I were of equal rank. He told me that, having been transferred suddenly from Africa to the high plateau, he didn't have the slightest idea of what our trench warfare was like.

"Don't worry," I told him, "because we know as little as you do."

"Do you think," he asked me, "that we'll be able to take the enemy positions?"

"If the Austrians leave," I replied, "there's a good chance that, in a couple of hours, after digging some passageways through the snow, we'll make it to the enemy trenches, although we may be frozen. But if the Austrians don't leave, I'd say it's highly unlikely."

"And will they leave?"

"Why should they leave?"

"And the bridges and ladders?"

"In this weather, they'll be extremely useful. Tonight we'll burn them to keep ourselves warm. Otherwise we'll all freeze to death."

The major wasn't in a joking mood. He was fully aware of the difficulties the battalion would run into during the assault. He was worried and irritated. And he found our brandy repugnant to boot.

The order to launch the attack hadn't arrived yet. Contrary to past experience, the hour had not been preestablished. The division commander had retained the prerogative to announce it at the last minute. Harmony of understanding.

An orderly from the regiment command came to call the major to report to the colonel. The major blanched and said to me, "This is it!"

And he walked off slowly, supporting himself with his walking stick, his legs sinking into the mud.

He was gone for half an hour. When he came back his face was beaming with joy. I saw him coming from a distance and couldn't discern the reason for the change.

Walking in the middle of the soldiers who let him go ahead, he exclaimed, "Nothing's going to happen tonight, nothing's going to happen tonight."

He walked over to me and shouted, "The operation has been suspended!"

"What do you mean, suspended?"

"Yes, suspended. The division commander has announced that the operation has been suspended. Apparently it was only supposed to be a demonstration. The general wishes to congratulate the troops for today's outstanding behavior."

The artillery was still firing. Maybe the general had forgotten to advise them that the operation had been suspended.

The units were told to go back to their shelters. They had been drinking before and they went on drinking afterward. Melancholy and joy are kindred emotions.

That night the major invited me to have dinner with him at the battalion command and, over coffee, he confided in me.

"I did the whole Libyan war and I fought in a lot of battles. I was awarded a medal of valor, as you can see, and I don't think I'm afraid of anything. I don't think I'm afraid of anyone anymore. I'm a career officer and there's a good chance that I'll be promoted to an even higher rank. But I can assure you that the most satisfying moments of my career have been like this one today. We are professional soldiers and we have no right to complain if we have to fight. But when we're ready to go into battle and, at the last minute, the order arrives to stand down, believe me, I'm telling you, you can be as brave as you want, but nothing makes you feel better than that. Honestly, moments like these are the best thing war has to offer."

Night was falling in a glacial cold. The soldiers were freezing and there was no wood for the stoves. After a quick exchange of ideas among the officers, we decided to burn the better part of the bridges and ladders.

XXIV

The regiment was at rest near the village of Ronchi. The command was higher up, in Campanella, at about five hundred meters. The three battalions were quartered in barracks and in the few houses still intact. The soldiers were tired. After monthlong rotations in the trenches, these rest periods of just a few days, under fire from enemy artillery, had gotten them down. But there was some hope of a longer rest. They had told us that this time that we were going down to the plains of the Veneto to finish up the winter. The distribution of new underwear and personal items seemed like certain confirmation and cheered up even the most discontent. Yet another event in the military hierarchy: I was promoted to captain.

Like our battalion commander, Major Frangipane, the commander of the 2nd Battalion, Major Melchiorri, had also arrived from Africa. We officers of the battalion invited him to lunch at our mess. It was the tradition among battalions to invite newly arrived officers to lunch, so we could get to know each other. The major was pleased to accept our invitation.

But that was not a day for ceremonies. The regiment

received the order to prepare to go back into the trenches. We were all dismayed. Good-bye, dreams of a long rest down on the plains!

Major Melchiorri still wanted to have lunch with us. When we all met at the mess, the soldiers had long since consumed their ration and returned to their quarters.

During lunch, the conversation was mainly about the colonial wars and the Great War. In the end, the two majors did all the talking and the rest of us listened. Major Frangipane had been in Libya for three years, Major Melchiorri in Eritrea for four or five. None of us had been in the colonies. What's more, except for Avellini, we were all reserve officers. I was sitting next to Major Melchiorri.

"The European war," he was saying, "will not be won until our troops are organized with the same disciplinary method that we used in the colonies to organize the Ethiopian askari. Obedience must be blind, as was justly required by the regulations of the glorious Piedmontese army, which Rome then decided to abolish. The masses must obey with their eyes closed and hold themselves honored to serve their fatherland on the battlefield."

"Our soldiers," our major responded, "are all citizens just like me and you; the askari are foreign mercenaries. This difference seems essential to me."

"The differences aren't great. Differences only exist in civilian life. Once he has put on the uniform, the citizen ceases to be such and loses all of his political rights. He is nothing but a soldier and has nothing but military duties. The superiority of the German Army consists in the fact that its soldiers come much closer to the model soldier typified by the askari. German officers command."

"What do you mean by command? I've had a fair amount of experience and I've got a pretty clear idea of how things are. In a war, when I receive an order, I'm consumed by the worry that it might be a mistake. I've seen a lot of them! And when I myself give an order, I think about it for a long time, for fear of making a mistake. To command means knowing how to command. That is, to avoid an accumulation of errors for which our soldiers are demoralized and sacrificed in vain."

"Commanders are never wrong and they never make mistakes. To command means having the right as a superior officer to give an order. There are not good orders and bad orders, or just orders and unjust orders. All orders are the same. An order is the absolute right to the obedience of others."

"That, dear colleague, might be the way to command a nice broomstick, if you've got one in hand. But you'll never be able to command Italian, French, Belgian, or English units that way."

"Because you have brought philosophy into the army. That's the reason for our decline."

As the conversation proceeded, fueled by numerous bottles, we could hear a noise rising up outside that sounded like the wind blowing against the doors, windows, and walls of the wooden barracks. The two majors stopped talking and we all listened. The noise was an uproar of shouting voices. Major Frangipane stood up and we all did the same. The door opened and the battalion duty officer came in. He was beside himself.

"There's been a mutiny! The Second Battalion started it and the others have followed. The units have left their quarters, shouting. Some officers have been beaten up."

Without waiting for an order from the major, we rushed outside to our units. My company's barracks, the closest to the mess, was reachable in just a few steps by passing through the kitchen. Followed by my junior officers, I took that route in a hurry, and in no time I was in the midst of the company.

The 10th was in a single wooden barrack that held all four platoons. It had a long center corridor for muster with two rows of double-decker beds on the sides. The soldiers, in small groups, were all in the corridor, arguing heatedly. When I entered, the officers were all behind me, and it was a soldier who first saw me and shouted everyone to attention. In the entire barrack you couldn't hear so much as a whisper.

I barked, "Company, fall in, rifles in hand."

The soldiers scrambled to get into place and obey the order. My thinking was: If the soldiers are beating up on officers and I order them to arms, I won't run the risk of being clubbed. If they have their arms in hand, they'll think more before they act, and, at worst, I'll run the risk of being shot. I must say I preferred being killed to being beaten.

Instantly, the platoons were in line with their rifles, in muster formation. The senior officer gave the order to stand at attention and presented the company. I gave the order to insert their bayonets and shoulder their rifles. The order was promptly executed. I called the roll; nobody was absent. If everyone was present then my company had not mutinied. Satisfactions are all of a personal nature and each of us is free to take them as he likes. I remember the pleasure I felt in that moment as one of the great pleasures of my life. Soldiers don't mutiny against a commander of a regiment, brigade, division, or army corps. When they rebel, they rebel against the officers in command of their own unit.

Outside, in the darkness, the turmoil was growing.

"We want a rest!"

"To hell with the war!"

"To hell with the trenches!"

The quarters of the 1st and 2nd Battalions were farther away, a couple of hundred meters from ours. The noise of a crowd on the march was coming from their direction. Probably the two battalions had joined up and were demonstrating together. I sent an officer to get a better idea of what was happening. He came back right away. The units had left their quarters unarmed, but they were destroying anything they found in their path.

"Down with the war!" Thousands of voices were shouting in unison.

I said a few words to the company, more to break the silence, which was hanging over us like a nightmare, than to give a speech. Besides, right then I had precious little to say and I realized that the units' attention was focused on the demonstrators. The major came in, followed by his adjutant and the battalion orderlies. I had the men present arms and I reported that all the men were present. The major was intensely emotional.

"Boys! Boys! What a day! . . ."

And he couldn't manage to say anything else. He left and I accompanied him outside the door. He told me that two platoons from the 9th under Lieutenant Avellini were in order; of the other two platoons quartered in another barrack there was still no news. The 11th was in chaos and the 12th was getting back into order after the arrival of its commander. The major was going around trying to persuade the rebels to get the whole battalion back together as soon as possible and get it away from the rebellion.

He went off in the direction of the 11th, and I walked out to the road. It was a dark night, but the light glowing from some windows illuminated the road. At the far end of it, a compact throng was advancing. The soldiers were all mixed together, with no division into units. Nobody was carrying a rifle. They were coming toward us, shouting and throwing stones at the windows of the administrative barracks. Two carts from the battalion, which had been sitting on the side of the road, were turned over and smashed to pieces.

"We want a rest!"

"To hell with the war!"

"No more lies!"

The column was advancing toward us. I went back inside. What was going to happen?

The uproar was growing. The head of the column came to a halt in front of our barracks.

"Out with the tenth!"

"Come out!"

"Comrades, everybody out!"

"Comrades, all together!"

"Out, out!"

There was no answer from the company.

In the crowd, a lone voice cried out, "Forget about them!"

The shouting continued for a few minutes. The column seemed to hesitate. It resumed the march, changed direction, and disappeared behind the barracks, on the road that led to the regiment command, to Campanella. I went over to the opposite side of the barrack and opened a window. A cold north wind was coming down out of the Campomulo valley and its howls accompanied the march into the Ronchi valley. I watched.

Down a narrow road that was as a kind of shortcut between the regiment command and the battalions, I could see a single file of lights. Surely this was the regiment's general staff that was coming toward us, lighting the way with lanterns. If they picked up the pace they would run right into the mass of demonstrators on the main road. The lights stopped and, from that same point came the blare of a trumpet, which drowned out the howling wind and the shouting from the demonstrators. The trumpet sounded "officer's call." The tune blared again, high and long. When the bugle fell silent, the shouting from the crowd ceased as well. The trumpet's appeal was greeted by the silence of the night. For a minute there was no sign of life in the valley. Then its echo, in the distance, toward Foza, Stoccaredo, Col Rosso, and the barracks of the Alpine brigade, sounded the notes again, repeated them, stretching them out—a sad wailing throughout the entire Asiago basin.

Why was the colonel calling us to report? Why was he calling the officers away from their units? Maybe it was to give a sign of life, a demonstration that the command was still there. I didn't intend to send my officers away from the company and sent only one to report.

The column of demonstrators came to a halt. I saw it as a big, teeming, black mass out on the road. The colonel waited for a few seconds, called off the report, and advanced toward the soldiers with his lantern in hand. When he reached them, their ranks opened and he passed between them. He raised his lantern so everyone could see his face and in a loud voice said, "For your own good, your colonel orders you to go back to your quarters."

From the lines in the back a voice responded, "We have the right to rest!"

The colonel replied, "We all have the right to rest. I'm old and I have the right to rest, too. But now go back to your quarters. Your colonel, for your own good, is ordering you to obey."

The crowd wavered. The first lines withdrew.

The commander of the 6th cried out, "Sixth company, muster in the barracks!"

Other officers followed suit and tried to round up their units. The front ranks of the crowd all began to break up. Only in the rear did the mass remain immobile as isolated shouts continued to protest.

The colonel crossed the road. Informed that the 10th Company was in formation with arms at the ready, he directed himself toward my barrack. When he came in, the shouting outside started back up again.

"We want a rest!"

"To hell with the war!"

The colonel did not respond to the company, which was presenting arms, and asked me, "Can I count on your company?"

"Certainly," I replied, "the company is in order."

"Can I count on your company if I give you the order to go back into the trench immediately?"

"Yes, sir."

"And can I count on your company if I give the order to intervene against the mutineers?"

The dialogue between the colonel and me was taking place in front of the entire company. We were almost at the center of the company, which was lined up in double file, and the muster formation allowed me to see the faces of half of the units. The soldiers were looking straight at me, staring.

I answered, "Colonel, I don't think so, sir."

"Give me a straight answer. Yes or no?"

"No, sir, colonel."

The colonel left the barrack. Outside, the uprising continued.

XXV

By ten o'clock, all the units of the three battalions were back in their quarters. Order had been reestablished. At midnight, we officers of the 3rd Battalion were still meeting, in the mess. The major and his adjutant were at the regiment command. Also missing were the officers assigned to night duty, one per company. We were discussing the evening's events among ourselves. Avellini was bound to all of us by such a feeling of camaraderie that there was no difference between him, a career officer, and us, reserve officers. That conversation is still present in my memory. I can summarize it as follows:

Ottolenghi: My unit was in order, or more or less in order. There was just one idiot who wanted to go outside and shoot his machine gun off into the air. I said to him, "One move and I'll shoot you." One machine gun? If the machine guns have to go out, they all go out. If my machine-gun unit rebels, it rebels all together, with the officers, the NCOs, the corporals, and the soldiers. In that case, I'll be part of the mutiny. And, one day or another, I thinks that's what's going to happen. Because I feel exactly the same way as the men who mutinied. They're right, a thousand times right, they just chose the wrong moment. Mutiny at night, and unarmed! What a dumb move!

Avellini: You're crazy as a loon.

Commander, 12th Company: Out of your mind.

Ottolenghi: If you're going to mutiny, you've got to do it in the daytime and with weapons, and take advantage of a good opportunity, so you can be sure everybody's in on it. Not one junior officer should be left out.

Commander, 12th Company: Great plan. And what about the others?

Ottolenghi: What others? I trust you don't want to mutiny together with the officers from the general staff.

Commander, 12th Company: If that's how you see it, then resign your commission.

Ottolenghi: Officer or soldier, military service is obligatory. And since there's no way to get out of it, I prefer to go to war as an officer.

Avellini: You swore an oath when you became an officer. Either what you're saying now isn't serious, or the oath you swore then wasn't serious.

Ottolenghi: The answer is obvious: the oath wasn't serious. Whether you're an officer or a soldier, you're forced to swear, individually or collectively. If you don't swear as an officer you have to swear as a soldier. It all comes down to the same thing. In our country, the only men exempt from military service are cardinals and bishops. The oath is nothing more than a formality that we are forced to perform by compulsory military service.

Avellini: A man of honor doesn't give his word knowing that he's lying.

Commander, 12th Company: Not only are you nuts, you're also a shady character.

Ottolenghi: Let's get this straight. Somebody takes you by force, against your will, weapon in hand, and forces you to take an oath. And you're telling me you dishonor yourself if you swear with the intention of not observing the oath?

Avellini: So who forced you? Nobody can force you to disobey your conscience.

Commander, 12th Company: If you've got one.

Ottolenghi: Nobody? In wartime, once you're drafted, if you refuse to take the oath you get court-martialed and the first chance they get they execute you. In a situation like that taking an oath is a necessary lie, an act of legitimate self-defense. Given that's the case, since there's no way out of it, I prefer to be an officer rather than a soldier.

Avellini: How come?

Ottolenghi: Sooner or later a favorable an opportunity will present itself, and when it does, I want to have the strength to act on a moment's notice.

A second lieutenant: Drink your wine and go to bed.

Ottolenghi: When that time comes, It won't just be my rifle and my bayonet, but a hundred rifles and a hundred bayonets. Plus, and, here's to your health, a pair of machine guns.

Commander, 11th Company: And who will you use the weapons against?

Ottolenghi: Against all the commands.

Commander, 11th Company: And then? Are you planning to take over as Supreme Commander?

Ottolenghi: All I'm planning to do is give the command to fire. On day X, sights down, fire at will! And I'd like to start with the division commander, whoever it happens to be, because they are all, inevitably, one worse than the other.

Commander, 11th Company: And then?

Ottolenghi: Onward and upward, right up the hierarchy. Ever onward, with order and discipline. That is, onward in a manner of speaking, because our real enemies are not beyond our own trenches. So first, about-face, then onward, ever onward.

A second lieutenant: That is, rearward.

Ottolenghi: Naturally. Ever onward, onward, all the way to Rome. That's where the enemy's general headquarters is.

Commander, 11th Company: And then?

Ottolenghi: Isn't that enough for you?

A second lieutenant: That ought to be one nice little pilgrimage.

Ottolenghi: Then? The government will be in the hands of the people.

Commander, 10th Company: So I guess you think that if our army marches on Rome, the German Army and the Austrians are going to stay put in their trenches? Or is it that , in order to please our new people's government, the Germans will go back to Berlin and the Austro-Hungarians to Vienna and Budapest?

Ottolenghi: I'm not interested in knowing what the others will do. All I want to know is what I want to do.

Commander, 10th Company: That's easy enough, but it doesn't solve the problem. What would it really mean, your march to the rear? A military victory for the enemy, obviously. And can you really hope that a military victory wouldn't also amount to a political victory over the defeated? Look at our wars for independence. Every time the enemy won, didn't they bring with them, on the points of their bayonets, the Bourbons to Naples and the popes to Rome? When the Austrians beat us, in Milan, and in Lombardy and Venetia, was it the people's government they left in or brought to power? When our enemies have been victorious, they have brought Italy under foreign domination and reactionary rule. Is that what you want?

Ottolenghi: Of course not. But neither do I want this war, which is nothing more than a miserable slaughter.

Commander, 10th Company: And your revolution, isn't that a slaughter, too? Isn't it a war, too, a civil war?

Commander, 11th Company: Honestly, I'd rather not have the one or the other.

Commander, 10th Company: But not Ottolenghi. He denounces the one and exalts the other. But aren't they really one and the same?

Ottolenghi: No, they're not one and the same. In a revolution you can see the progress of the people and of all the oppressed. In war, there's nothing except useless slaughter.

Commander, 10th Company: Useless? There are several of us here who have been to university. At my university we burned the speeches of Wilhelm II who, every chance he got, invoked the God of War, and who fed his subjects on nothing but bayonets and cannons. Useless slaughter? If we hadn't opposed the Central Powers, today, in Italy and the rest of Europe, we'd all be marching the goose step to the beat of a drum.

Ottolenghi: They're all the same.

Commander, 12th Company: And democracy? And freedom? Where would your people be without them?

Ottolenghi: Some democracy! Some freedom!

Commander, 10th Company: But democracy and freedom are why a lot of us favored intervention, answered the call to arms, faced all the sacrifices, and are getting ourselves killed.

Ottolenghi: The sacrifice doesn't make up for the slaughter.

Commander, 12th Company: And what about the interests of Italy?

Ottolenghi: And who are we? Aren't we Italy?

Commander, 10th Company: Have the ideals that drove us into war lost their value because the war is a slaughter? If we are convinced that we have to fight, our sacrifices are worth something. Sure, we're all tired, and the soldiers have proclaimed it to us loud and clear today. That's human. After a while, you get discouraged, start thinking only of yourself. The instinct for self-preservation takes over. And most of us would like to see the war end, no matter how, because the end of the war means the end of the threat to our lives. But is that enough to justify our desire? If that were so, wouldn't a handful of war mongers have us forever under their thumb just because we're afraid of a slaughter? What would become of world civilization if violent injustice were always able to impose itself without resistance?

Ottolenghi: I'll admit that if you want.

Commander, 10th Company: What you have to admit is that you have to defend the morality of your own ideas, even if it means risking your life. The weariness and the horrors are not a valid argument for condemning war. Tonight, our soldiers mutinied. Are they right or wrong? Maybe they're wrong, maybe they're right. Maybe both. The mass of men see nothing but the immediate present. But what would happen if their conduct were to be taken as the norm for conduct in the army?

Ottolenghi: They're revolt is legitimate because the incompetence of our superiors is what has made this war into the unbearable slaughter we see every day.

Commander, 11th Company: He's right about that.

Commander, 12th Company: Yes, on that, Ottolenghi is right.

A group of second lieutenants: That's for sure.

Avellini: Even I can't deny that.

Ottolenghi: You see? Even you are forced to admit I'm right.

Commander, 10th Company: When we entered the war our political and military leaders were unprepared. But that doesn't mean we should throw down our arms.

Ottolenghi: It seems to me that our generals were sent to us by the enemy to destroy us.

A group of second lieutenants: He's right.

Commander, 11th Company: I'll say.

Ottolenghi: And they're surrounded by a gang of speculators, protected by Rome, who are buying and selling our lives.

You saw it the other day with the shoes that were distributed to the battalion. What great shoes! On the soles, in big, tri-colored letters, there was written "Viva l'Italia!" After a day in the mud, we discovered that the soles were made of cardboard, painted to look like leather.

A group of second lieutenants: That's right.

Commander, 12th Company: Unhappily, that's the way it is.

Ottolenghi: The shoes are nothing. What's really terrible is that they've also painted over our lives, stamped us with the name of the fatherland, and led us like sheep to the slaughter.

The door opened. The conversation stopped. Major Frangipane came in, followed by Major Melchiorri and two adjutants.

We all stood up.

"I have proposed," Major Melchiorri said, "that ten men from each company immediately be shot. A stern example has to be made."

"The death penalty cannot be used against soldiers who didn't use their weapons," our major responded.

"The division commander is also in favor of a mass execution."

We listened to the two majors without saying a word. Ottolenghi turned to us and said, "I'm in favor of the execution of the division commander."

Major Frangipane looked weary and sad.

"Go to sleep," he said to us. "One duty officer per company is enough. Tomorrow morning we'll be informed of the commander's decision.

XXVI

The regiment had gone back up to the trenches. The army corps commander had followed the advice of the brigade commander and rejected the proposal for the death penalty. Only seven men, NCOs and soldiers, were court-martialed and sentenced to imprisonment. They were then granted the opportunity to serve in other regiments on the front line in exchange for having their sentences commuted. The rotations between time in the trench and rest periods continued as before.

As the spring sunshine gradually warmed up the mountains, the snow began to melt and recede. And as the level of the snow went down, so did the parapets of our trenches. The grand bastions lost their towers and the scaffolding was dismantled. Each week, we took down one row of bags filled with snow, and the loophole line slowly went back down to ground level.

Along with the nice weather came plans for new operations. Batteries of various caliber sprouted up all over the place, just like mushrooms. The whole wreath of peaks at our backs, crowning the Asiago basin, was an uninterrupted chain of camouflaged artillery batteries. The field and mountain batteries closest to us were merely the advance guard of that grand array of gaping barrels. This time the big guns were being deployed. More batteries, built during the winter, continued to arrive along the roads from Congo and Foza. Batteries of trench mortars were installed behind the front line. Day and night, long columns of trucks, loaded with munitions, rolled up the mountain roads from the plains of the Veneto. The corps of engineers worked to fill two large mines with gelignite: one under Casara Zebio, the other at 1496 meters, toward Mount Interrotto. Active war was once again announcing its arrival. But in April, although the snow had receded back up the sides of the basin, it was still quite high around all of our positions.

My battalion was at rest, on one of the usual rotations, in Ronchi. Major Frangipane, wounded by shrapnel when we were in the trench, was now in the hospital, and I was in command of the battalion.

Lieutenant Ottolenghi came to me to ask for authorization to go on an excursion with the battalion's squad of skiers. Still commander of the battalion's machine-gun section, he had nothing to do with the skiers. But, during the winter, for our own pleasure, we had practiced a lot together and had become good on skis. He had become a fanatic.

The battalion's skiers constituted a special squad under the command of a sergeant. They had taken an official course in Bardonecchia and, in accordance with the general directives on mountain warfare, they were supposed to provide patrols for reconnaissance missions beyond our lines. But the distances between our trenches and the enemy's were so small that there wasn't enough room for a ski patrol to operate in. The few attempts that were made had counseled against using them at night. In addition, the terrain had become so cluttered with uprooted trees and barbed wire that it was difficult to move through it. During the day, there wasn't a single point where our patrols could go out unobserved, and at night, on rare occasions, we sent out men on snowshoes. But the next day the tracks they left were highly visible and made the enemy even more vigilant.

The result of all this was that the ski squad was of no practical use whatsoever. The battalion commander used to send them out regularly on excursions to Campomulo, Croce di Longara, Mount Fior, and Foza, to keep them in training, but they had never been deployed beyond our lines.

Ottolenghi had participated in some of those excursions with me. So his request was in line with our winter routine. On the other hand, there were some operational matters to be taken care of, so I told him he could only take half a squad with him.

"No," he told me. "With half a squad I can't do anything worthwhile. What I'd like to do with the skiers is a proper live-war exercise, including launching hand grenades and petards. I'd like to be able to use the whole squad because that's the only way we can stage a complete patrol operation. We're on the eve of a big attack operation; I'd really like to help prepare our skiers for it, they're a fine squad of specialists."

I also had a strong interest in that kind of exercise and so I gave in. Ottolenghi headed off with the full squad: ten men, a corporal, and a sergeant. Their haversacks were loaded with bombs. Later, I was given a full rundown of the excursion.

"The order from our battalion commander," Ottolenghi told the skiers, "is to carry out a live-war operation, rapid and secret. This way, you'll be put to the test. Very soon, we're going to launch a large operation and we have to be adequately prepared. This time, we're going to be executing a serious attack; there'll be no bridges and ladders. A war operation like the one we've been ordered to carry out today requires an enemy. Where is our enemy? That is the question. The Austrians? Obviously not. No, our natural enemies are our generals. If His Excellency General Cadorna were here in the vicinity, he would be our main enemy, and all we'd have to do is track him down. Unfortunately, he is not anywhere near here. And neither is the commander of our army. Even the commander of our army corps is far away, hiding out at the foot of the high plateau. The big generals hate the snow. So who's left? All we've got left are the small fry. What we have is our division commander, small but perfect. A rare intelligence. A rare intelligence, indeed."

The skiers knew Ottolenghi very well. His reputation had spread throughout the battalion long ago. They found him entertaining.

"But in any case," the sergeant asked, somewhere between serious and facetious, "we're not . . . we're certainly not going to use these bombs to attack the general in command of our division, are we?"

"Not directly," Otolenghi replied "We aren't going to attack the honorable general personally, even though that would constitute, beyond any doubt, a remarkable step toward victory. The battalion commander's orders are: 'Do whatever you like, but spare the life of the general.' So we're going to obey. We're going to spare his life, but we're going to attack his property. We're going to carry out a bold, lightning-fast raid on the division supply depot, plundering as much of it as we possibly can."

The skiers couldn't have been more enthusiastic. Ottolenghi explained to them all the details of the plan he had painstakingly designed. Then they headed off to execute it, with Ottolenghi leading the way.

The supply depot was in a big wooden barrack, along the road between Campomulo and Foza, tucked into a small hollow that kept it hidden from enemy observers. The snow around it was very deep. Ottolenghi and the skiers knew the area well from having passed nearby on previous excursions. The depot held a plentiful supply of foodstuffs for the troops and for the officers' messes of all the units in the division. There was also and abundant stockpile of wine and liqueurs, dry-cured hams, mortadella sausages, salamis, and cheeses.

The squad made a wide circle to surprise the depot from above and render unrecognizable the direction of approach of their ski tracks. Just before sunset, they arrived all together at a point about one kilometer above the road. From there, still all together, they began their descent toward the depot. When they got to within several hundred meters, the patrol split into two squads baptized by Ottolenghi as the "tactical," composed of himself, the sergeant, and six soldiers, and the "logistical," composed of four soldiers and the corporal.

The first squad was supposed to attack from the front, in the face of the depot, the second from the back.

The first squad took off in descent, launching grenades and petards and yelling. Their cries and the explosions attracted the attention of the soldiers minding the depot. They all rushed outside. What they saw was an extraordinary spectacle. The skiers accompanied the launch of the explosives with nimble circling maneuvers, zipping through the clouds created by the exploding smoke bombs and grenades, making it seem like there were two patrols, one right after the other, skiing furiously. The peace-loving soldiers who worked in the depot didn't realize that the petards, which exploded on the surface of the snow, were all "offensive" and therefore almost totally innocuous to those who launched them, and that the more dangerous bombs exploded much farther away, down low, deep under the snow. It was an exceptional and real view of war. The soldiers from the depot, used to working in supply dumps behind the lines, had never seen combat before. For a few minutes, it seemed to them that those crazy combatants were heroically going to blow each other to shreds right before their eyes. Then their admiration gave way to shuddering horror.

As the battle raged before the astonished eyes of the custodians of the depot, the "logistical" squad, at the back, went to work a little less audaciously. The five men, their skis unlatched, jumped through the windows into the depot and came out loaded. Ottolenghi had outfitted them with haversacks

Alpine packs, and ropes. They came back out of the windows stuffed and covered with hams, mortadella sausages, salamis, and bottles. After relatching their skis, they vanished into the valley on the other side of the Ronchi.

The bold operation had succeeded brilliantly in every respect.

That evening, at mess, Ottolenghi offered us four bottles of Barbera, for his grandfather's saint's day. His grandfather? I thought to myself. The next morning, I started having my first doubts.

An urgent phonogram from the division command recounted what had happened and ordered all of its subordinate commands to conduct investigations to discover the guilty parties. The general demanded that such "banditry" be punished without pity. I had just finished reading the phonogram when word arrived that Sergeant Melino, from the 10th Company, had been wounded, struck in the leg by shrapnel from a grenade. The medical officer had treated him and put him on rest for a week. Melino was none other than the sergeant of the ski squad. He was a veteran of my company and I had promoted him to lance corporal, corporal, and sergeant. I had personally selected him for the skiing course in Bardonecchia and I had the utmost trust in him. I went to see him. His leg was bandaged and he was lying down.

"The battalion is at rest," I said to him, "and you get yourself wounded by a grenade? You want to explain that wound to me?"

There were some soldiers nearby and the sergeant made

me understand that they should be sent away. I had them leave the room.

"What's all this mystery about?" I asked.

The sergeant told me the whole story. The hams, the mortadella sausages, the salamis, and the vast assortment of bottles had all been distributed that same night to the squads of the battalion, in secret, by way of the skiers who belonged to the various companies. In all likelihood, there was nothing left of the loot. Things might well get complicated. I called the medical lieutenant and had him suspend the official communication of the sergeant's wound. Afterwards, I interrogated Ottolenghi.

"Since when," I said to him, "have revolutions been made by stealing hams and mortadella sausages?"

"Stealing has always been part of revolutions."

"Hams?"

"Hams, too."

"That was some operation you had the battalion carry out. Read this phonogram from the division commander. Read this report on Sergeant Melino's wound. How do you think the battalion can get itself out of this mess?"

"What do you want to do?" he asked. "The battalion's reputation will only benefit from this operation. You can't deny it. It was magnificent. If I had had a platoon with me I could have emptied out the entire depot, including the coffee and sugar. What do you say we repeat it against the division commander in person? Do you want to? Tell me, do you want to? Nobody will ever know, I promise you. He'll be taken prisoner. It'll be a total secret. The soldiers will be delighted to have a little distraction. What do you say?"

I called the officers to report. I read them the phonogram from the division and ordered an immediate investigation. A few hours later, I received a written report on the results. Negative. The unit commanders ruled out the possibility that their subordinates could have taken part in or witnessed the event. Ottolenghi's report was also negative.

Shortly before mess time, I ran into Avellini and asked him, "Off the record, just between us, do you know anything about this story of the division supply depot?"

"My men were eating ham and salami all night long. Some of them got indigestion. They must have been dying of thirst. I had some flasks of wine brought in because apparently the stolen bottles weren't enough to go around."

The report of the regiment command was negative, too.

XXVII

Intensive preparations were under way for a great offensive. It was certain that our brigade would have an important role. Topographical charts of the region, as far as Peak XII and Val Lagarina, were distributed to the officers. Every so often, isolated cannon shots announced that the new batteries were adjusting their range. The positioning of the heavy mortars had also been completed. Our sector of the regiment alone numbered twenty or so batteries, arranged in groups.

To compensate the troops for their winter fatigue and motivate them for the offensive, the brigade was sent on a rest rotation, down on the plains. Our battalion was quartered in Vallonara, at the foot of the high plateau.

The rest didn't last very long, only eight days. But that one week was magic. For more than a year, since Aiello, the soldiers had not lived in the midst of the civilian population. Their weariness and discontent vanished in a flash and, for the benefit of the civilians, everyone adopted an air of confidence and martial protection. Weren't we the saviors of the fatherland? If we hadn't gone to fight, wouldn't the people have had to abandon their homes and their fields and migrate, in desperation, to the hinterland, only to live in misery on the paltry subsidies begrudgingly handed out by the state? The young girls gazed at the soldiers with such admiration!

For our battalion, those were some of the most delightful days of the war. The soldiers were happy. Vallonara was a town of a few hundred inhabitants, but the rich countryside between Bassano and Marostica was sprinkled with thousands of dairy farms. During the hours of free time, they became the meeting places, cheerful and gay, for squads or isolated groups of soldiers. The local population and the soldiers engaged in a reciprocal contest of generosity. Everything the soldiers possessed was offered for the festivities. They became, in those hours, the lords of the plains. Every company had its share of sedentary soldiers. Meditative and solitary, they were insensitive to that life of jollity. They didn't even go outside and, misanthropes that they were, idled away their time in and around their quarters. But the younger soldiers roved about the countryside like wandering knights, searching for a sip of joy. On the warm, red afternoons of that enchanted May, the whole company resounded with ditties and popular songs. And the voices of the soldiers, no longer grave, harmonized with the songs of the merrymaking women. Life was beautiful again!

One day, walking along a row of grapevines to check a battalion phone wire, I tripped over a soldier from the 10th Company. He was with a young farm girl. Lying on the grass, under an arch of vines, they were exchanging secrets. I hadn't noticed they were there; otherwise I would have avoided them. Our meeting was a surprise, for me and for them. The soldier leaped to his feet, at attention, and saluted. He was red in the face and confused. At his side, slowly, slowly, with a graceful calm, the woman, too, raised herself up on her feet. Slender and blonde, she looked even blonder next to the olive-skinned man with black hair. She glanced at me with a timid smile, lowered her eyes, and pressed against the soldier—the protectress.

I pulled out my wallet, took out a ten-lire note, and handing it to the soldier, said, "Your captain is proud to see one of his soldiers in such lovely company."

The soldier took the money, still embarrassed, and the young woman broke into a long smile, swaying back and forth, her big eyes open wide and full of grace. They were so happy they made me feel happy too.

Happy and unhappy at the same time. My sentimental situation, in fact, was still up in the air.

In those days, Lieutenant Avellini was in seventh heaven. The family in Marostica invited us often for tea, but I was still in command of the battalion and so busy with endless official duties, even in the afternoon hours, that I was able to go only rarely. He wasn't nearly as busy and never failed to make it.

A personal success added to his joy. The brigade commander had assigned him to give a lecture to the officers of the brigade on the tactical deployment of the company in mountain combat. He prepared with enthusiasm, and I helped him, too, giving him the benefit of my long experience in the war. We hated lectures even more than heavy artillery, but Avellini had a talent for speaking. The general congratulated him on his performance and recommended him to the division command as a distinguished career officer. He couldn't contain his joy. After the lecture, he shared some things with me in confidence. He loved nothing more than his military career. To be able to distinguish yourself as a company commander, be admitted to the War College and serve on the general staff, command an artillery battery, then an infantry battalion, and study, study, always study. To serve your country like that, helping to give it an army, a great army, so it could reaffirm its past military glories! It seemed he couldn't ask for anything more out of life.

That afternoon we went to Marostica together for tea and he was the guest of honor.

Our rest period went by like a dream.

XXVIII

On June 8, anticipating our offensive, the Austrians detonated the mine under Casara Zebio, the one for which we had spent Christmas night on the line. The mine destroyed the trenches, burying the units that were occupying them, together with the officers of a regiment that had stopped there during a reconnaissance mission. The event was interpreted as a sign of worse things to come.

On the tenth, our artillery opened fire at five in the morning. The great offensive, spread out over fifty kilometers, from Val d'Assa to Mount Caldiera, had begun. Counting the large-caliber trench mortars, there were no less than a thousand artillery pieces on the high plateau. An immense wave of drumfire, accented by deafening booms that sounded like they were erupting from the bowels of the earth, devastated the terrain. The earth itself trembled under our feet. That was not artillery fire; it was all hell broken loose. We had always complained about the lack of artillery; now we had it, in spades.

The units had been withdrawn from the trenches and only a few lookouts were left to man them. The 1st and 2nd Battalions took shelter in the big caves that had been dug out during the winter. The 3rd Battalion, with all four of its companies, was out in the open, in line with the two rear-guard redoubts. The small caves nearby were occupied by the mountain artillery, which had its battery there, and by our machine gunners.

The enemy artillery fired back at our batteries with big-caliber guns, but they didn't fire on our front line. The only fire against our front line came from our own artillery.

What happened was never adequately clarified. Some 149mm and 152mm marine batteries fired on us. The battalions that were in the caves suffered no casualties, but mine had serious losses right from the start. Major Frangipane, who had returned to duty just a few days before, was among the first to be hit, and I took over command of the battalion. The line of the two small redoubts, in which my battalion had been ordered to stay, was leveled. They had been built to withstand fire from the front, not from the rear. The 9th and 10th Companies were cut in half. Lieutenant Ottolenghi ordered his machine gunners out of the caves and, after realigning them out in the open, cried out, "We have to march on the batteries that are firing on us and machine gun them!"

I saw him in time, ran over to him, and made him go back to his position. I had the companies move a few hundred meters to the rear and informed the regiment command of our new position. The battalion already had a lot of dead soldiers. The stretchers were insufficient to transport all the wounded to the first-aid stations.

As I was shuttling between units, a colonel from the artillery passed by, followed by two lieutenants. Bareheaded, pistol in hand, surrounded by exploding grenades, he yelled out, "Kill us! Kill us!"

I went over to him and proposed that he use my officers to communicate to his batteries the order to adjust their range. He didn't even realize that I was an officer. He didn't answer me and kept on yelling disconnected phrases. The two lieutenants followed him, mute, staring into space. I started to lose my composure. In preparation for the attack, the brigade command had set up nearby, behind my battalion. I rushed over to it. I found the general in command of the brigade sitting in the back of a small cave, holding a microphone. I told him as fast as I could what was happening. He listened to me, calm to the point of enervation. My voice betrayed my agitation, but he remained indifferent.

In my excitement, I couldn't keep myself from saying, "General, sir, we're just going from one blunder to another out there today!"

The general sprang to his feet. I thought he was going to throw me out. He came over to me and threw his arms around me, crying. "Son, that's our profession," he replied.

I learned that he had been sending dispatches and phonograms, in vain, for over an hour. I went back to my battalion, desperate. In the 2nd Battalion's sector, even worse things were happening. Major Melchiorri had installed himself in a small cave, next to the big cave where the 5th Company was sheltered. The artillery fire had shaken him. A colonist, he had never seen anything like this in the African wars. His nerves were shot. He had already drunk, by himself, a full bottle of brandy and had sent out the entire staff of the battalion command to find him a second. He was still waiting for the bottle when a tumultuous uproar came from the 5th Company's cave.

This was the most poorly excavated of all the caves occupied by the regiment. It was one of the first to be dug, when the miners were still inexperienced. It was long horizontally, but not deep enough. It could hold an entire company, but there was very little room front to back. Capable of holding up under bombardment from small-caliber guns, it couldn't withstand bigger shells. Maybe it actually could have held up against big guns, too, but the men inside had the impression that it couldn't. That morning, our 149mm and 152mm guns had been concentrating their fire on it. Some shells had exploded near the mouth of the cave and killed two soldiers and the captain in command of the company. Entire batteries had continued to pummel it. Finally, the company, dazed from the uninterrupted bombardment, choking on the smoke from the exploding shells, and deprived of their commander, couldn't take it anymore. To the soldiers it seemed like the roof of the cave was about to collapse and crush them all. They wanted to get out from under. They were shouting, "We want out! We want out!"

Major Melchiorri heard the shouting and sent someone to find out what was happening. When he learned that the soldiers wanted to come out of the cave, he was overwhelmed by a surge of rage. His orders required that the units not move from their assigned positions until the hour established for the attack.

"We are in the face of the enemy," the major yelled, "and my orders are that nobody moves. Woe to anyone who moves."

The second bottle arrived and the major forgot about the 5th Company.

The shelling continued. It wasn't long before the company poured out of the cave and rearranged itself, out in the open, at the bottom of a lateral downslope, out of the artillery's range.

The major thought he was in the midst of a mutiny. He was sure of it. A company, minutes before an assault, its weapons in hand, just a few meters from the enemy, was refusing to obey. For him, there was no doubt. Therefore, he had to take the strongest possible measures to punish the sedition. Furious, he came striding out of his cave, had the company close ranks, and ordered its decimation.

The 5th Company obeyed the orders without objection. As the adjutant counted the soldiers and designated every tenth one for immediate execution, the news spread throughout the other units in the battalion and several officers rushed to investigate. The major explained to them that he intended to avail himself of the communiqué from the Supreme Command authorizing capital punishment with exceptional procedures. The commander of the 6th Company was among those present. He was Lieutenant Fiorelli, the old commander of the 6th Company during the August operation, who, healed of his wounds and promoted to captain, had reassumed command of the company. He pointed out that the crime of mutiny in the face of the enemy did not exist and that, even if the crime had been committed, the major would not have the right to order a decimation without approval from the regiment commander.

The captain's observations irritated the major. He took out his pistol and held it against the captain's chest.

"You be quiet," the major replied, "be quiet, otherwise you are an accomplice to a mutiny and guilty of the same crime. I and I alone am the commander in charge here. If the soldiers under my command violate the discipline of war in the face of the enemy, I am the sole judge over their life and death."

The captain remained imperturbable. Calmly, he asked several times for permission to speak. The major ordered him to remain silent.

The selection of the men from the 5th was completed, and twenty soldiers, detached from the others, stood in wait.

The major ordered everyone to attention and he himself stood at attention as well. The booming of the artillery was deafening and he had to scream to make himself understood. His tone was solemn.

"In the name of His Majesty the King, supreme commander of the army, I, Major Melchiorri, Cavalier Ruggero, titular commander of the 2nd Battalion, 399th infantry, avail myself of the special dispositions of His Excellency General Cadorna, his chief of staff, and order the execution of the soldiers of the 5th Company, guilty of armed mutiny in the face of the enemy."

By this point the major was enraptured and unable to pay attention to anything but his own voice. But his state of mind was completely out of touch with the other officers present, the 5th Company, and the twenty soldiers designated to die.

There had never been an execution in our brigade. This decimation appeared to be an event so precipitous and so extraordinary as not to be considered even possible. But everyone need not believe in the drama for it to be played out. Major Melchiorri now found himself at the center of the drama, as its already overwhelmed protagonist.

The major ordered Captain Fiorelli, with a platoon of his company, to take command of the execution platoon.

"I am the titular commander of a company," the captain responded, "and I cannot command a platoon."

"You are refusing, therefore, to obey my order?" the major asked.

"I am not refusing to obey an order. I am merely pointing out that I am a captain and not a lieutenant, the commander of a company and not of a platoon."

"Enough," shouted the major, once again pointing his pistol at the captain. "Are you or are you not going to obey the order I've given you?"

The captain responded, "No, sir."

"You're not going to obey!"

"No, sir."

The major had a moment's hesitation and didn't shoot the captain.

"Well then," the major resumed, "order a platoon from your company to form a line."

The captain repeated the order to the second lieutenant in command of the 1st Platoon of the 6th. In a few minutes the platoon came out of its cave and formed a line. The second lieutenant received from the major, and repeated to his men, the order to load their weapons. The platoon already had its weapons loaded. Facing them, immobile, stunned, the twenty stared back at them. The major gave the order to aim.

"Aim!" the lieutenant ordered.

The platoon raised their rifles and took aim.

"Give the order to fire," the major shouted.

"Fire!" the lieutenant ordered.

The platoon executed the order. But they fired high. The discharge from their rifles had passed so high over the heads of the condemned that they were all still in their places, impassive.

If the platoon and the twenty had been acting in concert, the twenty could easily have thrown themselves to the ground and pretended to be dead. But there hadn't been anything more between them than an exchange of glances. After the discharge, one of the twenty smiled. The major's wrath exploded. With his pistol in hand, he took a few steps toward the condemned, his face contorted with rage. He stopped halfway and yelled, "All right, I'll punish the rebels myself!"

He had time to fire three shots. After the first, a soldier struck in the head collapsed on the ground; after the second and third, two more soldiers fell, hit in the chest.

Captain Fiorelli took out his pistol. "Major, sir, you are insane."

The execution platoon, without an order, aimed their rifles at the major and fired. The major fell to the ground, riddled with bullets.

The assault was scheduled to begin in a few minutes. Even the 149mms and 152mms had adjusted their range and weren't shelling us anymore. Our trenches had been devastated. Of the lookouts left to guard them, not more than two or three were found still alive. But there were enormous breaches in the enemy trenches and entanglements, opening the way for the assault. My battalion was amassed in a trench. I watched the 5th and 6th Companies of the 2nd Battalion , followed by the 7th and 8th, climb over our trenches en masse and reach the enemy trenches. My battalion climbed out immediately afterward, farther to the right. The 1st Battalion and a battalion from the other regiment of our brigade also occupied enemy positions, which were full of dead bodies.

These were the only four battalions, from Val d'Assa to Mount Caldiera, to succeed in the assault. Along the rest of the front, the operation failed. The mine at 1,496 meters, on the division's far left flank, caved in on our troops, making the enemy positions inaccessible. Our casualties were enormous. I had begun the attack as a company commander and finished it as the commander of two battalions, the 3rd and the 1st, which was left with no captains.

Since the operation had failed except in our sector, our advanced position, with our flank exposed to enemy fire, became unsustainable. At nightfall we received the order to withdraw, back to the trenches we had left.

That night, Captain Fiorelli came to see me. He was totally disheartened. He recounted to me the death of Major Melchiorri, for which he, too, felt partly responsible. He told me he had done everything possible to be killed in combat. Fate had decided to spare him. He thus felt compelled to do his duty and report what had happened to the regiment command. I wasn't able to dissuade him. The next day, in writing, he reported himself. The brigade, regiment, division, and army corps commands were informed immediately. Fiorelli, the lieutenant adjutant of the second battalion, and the second lieutenant of the 6th, were remitted to the military tribunal and placed under arrest. The three officers, accompanied by a captain in the carabinieri and an escort, passed through the middle of my battalion. As they did, the soldiers stood at attention and saluted.

XXIX

I won't revisit or recount anything but what impressed me most.

The operation started back up on June 19, but my battalion, which had suffered the most casualties, stayed behind in brigade reserve and didn't take part in the battle.

The great majority of the wounded from the battalion were transported by ambulances from the division command back to hospitals behind the lines. Avellini, among the most gravely wounded, was still in a field hospital near Croce Sant'Antonio. He was not transportable. He had been seriously hurt in the enemy trenches, at the head of his company. He had lost an eye, but the worst damage was where he had been hit in the abdomen. Before the stretcher-bearers carried him away, he asked to speak to me, and I was able to see, even then, the gravity of his condition. He strained to pull himself up on the stretcher and immediately fainted and fell back down. I didn't see him again before he was taken away. Even though the battalion was behind the lines, my official duties kept me from going to visit him. I was able to telephone the director of the hospital every so often for news on how he was doing. His temperature was always high.

On June 22, the director called me to say that Avellini wanted to see me right away, that I shouldn't waste any time, because his condition was desperate. I asked for authorization from the regiment command and got permission to leave the battalion for a few hours.

How changed my friend was! He hadn't eaten since June 10; the abdominal wound had forced him into a total fast. Before, he had been so strong and full of life; now, he was incapacitated. Lying on a cot, his lips white, immobile, he looked like a corpse. Only a slight contraction of his mouth, like a bitter smile, showed that he was alive and suffering. I immediately felt that he was dying. And I thought about his dreams of a military career, his service on the general staff, his promotions, the great national army.... Poor Avellini! No doubt, he would still want to talk to me about all of that.

Both of his eyes were bandaged, so he couldn't see me when I came in. But he heard my footsteps and understood that it was me. With a voice so weak I could hardly hear it, he called me by name.

"Yes," I replied, "it's me. Don't talk. Don't tire yourself out. I'll do the talking. The doctor told me your chances are good. But you have to be sure not to wear yourself out. The whole battalion is thinking of you and wants to see you soon. But you should only be thinking about getting better. There's no hurry. Everybody says hello. Especially the soldiers in your company...."

"The soldiers?"

"Yes, the soldiers. I made it a point to stop by your company on my way here. The colonel says hello too, and I have some nice news to give you on his behalf."

"Thanks. Thanks. Let me talk. . . . It's over, you know. . . ."

"What are you talking about? Don't be silly. You have to think about getting better."

The slightest effort was painful for him. Even those few words he'd said had tired him out. His face was totally contracted in pain. I had some news for him that would please him. Maybe it would pick his spirits up.

"There's some good news for you. Guess . . ."

He gestured with his hand. Was it curiosity or indifference? I went on.

"You've been nominated for a Silver Medal for Military Valor . And you've also been proposed for a promotion to captain for Merit of War. The brigade commander has already expressed a favorable opinion. The two proposals will certainly be approved by the higher commands. That's what the colonel charged me to tell you."

He raised his emaciated hands and let them fall back down again with a look of impotence. It seemed as though he wanted to say: "What does all that matter?"

"I called you, you know, for this. . . . Stand by me like a brother. Let me talk."

He spoke with difficulty, in monosyllables.

"You remember, that packet of letters?"

"Sure, I remember it well."

"In my personal property box, at transport, you'll find two of them. You know who you have to send them to."

I forced myself to make a joke, to cheer him up a little, and said, "Those letters are good-luck charms. They brought you luck on the night of the mine. They'll bring you more luck now for your wounds."

"Yeah, yeah, they're good luck. You can send them. But I'd rather you delivered them personally. And that you added this one, too."

I hadn't noticed that on the bed, under his outstretched hand, there was a letter. He picked it up and showed it to me.

"Do me a favor, read it to me. Come closer, come closer to me."

I took the letter. I sat down next to the bed, close enough to touch his blankets. The envelope was still sealed. I asked, "So you want me to open it?"

"Yeah, yeah. But come closer to me."

I leaned against the side of the bed. I looked at the envelope. It was addressed to him and was postmarked Marostica. I was shaking. I opened it and took out two pages. I didn't dare read it.

He asked me, "Did you open it?"

"Yes."

"So read it, do me the pleasure."

I unfolded the pages and my gaze went right to the signature. It was the name of the blond woman. I started to read. My voice was shaking.

"Sweetheart . . ."

Avellini put his hands over his bandaged eyes, almost as though he wanted to hide his tears. He was crying. I stopped reading. I let him go on crying, without saying a word. After a few minutes, he said, "Go on, go on."

I continued reading. A woman can't write words more tender than the ones I read that day. I had to stop reading again, more than once, because Avellini could not stop crying.

"What do I care if I die, what do I care?"

I finished reading the letter. He begged me to read it to him a second time. And I reread it, stopping myself often, like before, so intense was my friend's emotion.

"Even death is beautiful . . ."

He took the letter in his hands and caressed it lovingly. He said to me, "Leave it here with me. You can come and get it after I die."

My leave time was up. I had to get back to the battalion. I didn't dare say any more about hope. Getting up, I asked him, "Should I say anything to the company? To the colonel?"

"Yes, yes, thanks."

He pulled me down close to him with his hands and said to me, "You go personally. I want you to go in person. Tell her that my last thought was of her. That I didn't think of anything but her. . . . Tell her that I died happy."

I hurried back up to the battalion. But I was so agitated that, once I got there, I kept on walking and went all the way up to the trenches. Only there did I realize that I had gone past my battalion's sector by more than a kilometer.

I had just gotten back to the battalion command when

I was called to the telephone. It was the director of the hospital. He went around and around to tell me that Avellini's condition had gotten worse, that it was grave, that there was no hope. In the end he told me that he was dead and had left a letter for me.

I left the command cabin. There were some officers and soldiers near the command. I didn't know what to say, didn't know what to do. Then I walked over toward the 9th Company. It seemed right to me that I be the one to communicate the sad news. The only officer who had survived the assault on June 10 was a second lieutenant, and he had taken over command of the company. He was really fond of Avellini. I was incapable of using euphemisms and told him directly, "Avellini died, a few minutes ago."

"Avellini's dead?" the second lieutenant asked.

"He's dead, just now," I replied.

"He's dead, he's dead . . . dead . . ."

Then it seemed to me that something unrelated to us and the news I'd just given him was bothering him, like an uncertainty. But that state of mind of his lasted only an instant. With a rapid gesture, he grabbed a bottle of brandy he had nearby and, as though it were medicine, bolted down a glass of it.

I was shocked and irritated.

"What?" I screamed at him. "What? I tell you that your company commander is dead, and you, in front of your battalion commander, take a drink, just like that? And you're an officer? An officer? You?"

The second lieutenant seemed to wake up from a dream. He answered me, confused.

"Excuse me, captain, sir. I drank without even realizing what I was doing, involuntarily. I just realized it now. I'm sorry."

I retraced my steps back to the command. Life seemed so sad. Avellini was gone now, too. Of my old comrades from the battalion, there was nobody left. Even Ottolenghi had been wounded, and seriously, on the tenth. I didn't even know which hospital he was in. Once again, I was the only one left. Everybody had gone, yet again. And now I had to look for letters, tell the story, explain. It's not true that the instinct of self-preservation is an absolute law of life. There are times when life weighs on you more than the expectation of death.

XXX

In mid-July, the brigade came down from the trenches for a rest. The battalion was quartered between Asiago and Gallio, along the Mount Sisemol back line, to work on some fortifications. We were still under fire from enemy artillery, but well protected in out-of-the-way ravines. Only some rare enemy reconnaissance planes flew over us, way up high, quickly driven off by the intervention of our fighter squadrons from the Bassano air fields. The bomber planes didn't disturb anything but our rest. Our days of tragedy were followed by some hours of joy. The men with light wounds came back to the battalion, and new arrivals, officers and soldiers, filled the voids that had been left in the units. After a long convalescence, Cavalry Lieutenant Grisoni was newly assigned to our battalion and assumed command of the 12th Company. Still limping from his wound on Mount Fior, he hadn't lost his sense of humor. His cheerful disposition was invaluable in helping to drive away our sadness. We soon started forgetting again. Life regained the upper hand. My orderly, another of the wounded, had come back from the hospital. He resumed his reading of the bird book and I went back to Baudelaire and Ariosto.

One day around sunset, I was on the main road from the Ronchi valley to Mount Sisemol, on my way back from the regiment command in Ronchi. About halfway, I met up with a colonel riding a sorrel horse, alone. I was on horseback, too, also alone. I saluted him and went on my way. I'd gone a little ways ahead when I heard my name called. I turned in the saddle; he was talking to me. I turned my horse around and went back to meet him.

"At your orders, colonel," I said.

"Come here. Don't you recognize your superiors anymore?"

It was Colonel Abbati. Does the reader remember the lieutenant colonel from the 301st Infantry in Stoccaredo on Mount Fior? It was him. The red ribbon under his stars indicated that he was the titular commander of a regiment.

"Pardon me, colonel," I said, "I didn't recognize you."

Actually, it would be hard to recognize him at first glance. He was infinitely thinner and much older. His amber pallor had become a lemon color and his eyes were sunk way back in their orbits. He looked tired and sick.

He asked me a few questions about my regiment and then said, "Have you started drinking?"

"Just as before, colonel, sir."

"I don't know anymore if that's good or bad. The question is more complicated than I used to think it was. Do you find me changed?"

"A little tired. You look a little tired, but not really all that changed."

"A little tired! I'm finished. It won't be long until they make me a general. General for Merit of Brandy. Colonel Abbati has managed to kill the meaning of the war, but brandy has killed Colonel Abbati."

"What do you mean, colonel, sir?"

"This is not the war of infantry versus infantry, artillery versus artillery. It's the war of canteen versus canteen, cask versus cask, bottle versus bottle. As for me, the Austrians have won. I declare myself defeated. Take a good look at me: I'm beaten. Don't you find that I have the look of a man defeated?"

"I find that you look fine on a horse, colonel, sir."

"I should have drunk water, too, and lots of coffee. But now it's too late. Coffee excites the spirit, but it doesn't set it afire. Liquor sets it afire. I've incinerated my brain. I've got nothing left inside my head but burnt ashes. I still stir them, stir up the ashes to find some live embers to light a fire. But there aren't any left. If only we still had some snow and ice. Even the cold has gone away. With this damn sun, all I can see is cannons, rifles, dead bodies, and the wounded screaming in pain. I keep looking for some shade to take refuge. But I haven't had any for a long time. So long, captain."

A few days later, around noon, I was at mess with the officers from my battalion. We were waiting for a second lieutenant from the 11th Company, who I had sent to the regiment command to pick up some equipment. The call to mess had already sounded and the lieutenant still hadn't arrived. We sat down to the table without him. The second lieutenant arrived just as we were finishing.

"You're half an hour late," our younger colleagues reprimanded him. "Buy us two bottles!"

"Does he have to buy?" asked the manager of the mess.

"Yes," all the officers responded in chorus.

"All right. Two bottles! But I want to tell you why I was late."

"That's not necessary," said Lieutenant Grisoni. "We'll settle for the two bottles."

"No, I want to tell you what happened to me."

The whole table sat and listened.

"I was on my way back from Ronchi on the road that runs along the river. The sun was burning hot. When I got within sight of the white church, at the point where the trees cover the road, I saw a man on horseback, moving slowly, trying to stay out of the sun. When he got to the trees, in the shade, the horse stopped. The man stood up on the saddle, climbed up onto a tree limb, and disappeared among the foliage. All I could see was the horse, standing still. I kept out of sight. After a few minutes, the man reappeared, sticking out from the branches, but with his head down, hanging by his legs. I was stunned. But I thought: It must be someone who likes to do gymnastics. Though it seemed strange to me that someone would want to do gymnastics like that. I was still out of sight. Neither the horse nor the man had noticed me. The man dropped down into the saddle, standing on his hands, and then got back into the normal position for a man on horseback. He relaxed, took out his canteen, and took a drink. He put the canteen away and started over again. He climbed up onto a limb, disappeared, and reappeared after a few minutes, with his head down. He got back in the saddle and took another drink. I stayed there, out of sight, for around half an hour. The road was deserted. He repeated the operation three times. I wanted to get closer to see better, but just then a horse cart came trotting down the road. The man spurred his horse and rode off."

"Was the horse a sorrel?" I asked.

"Yes, a sorrel."

"Two white socks?"

"Two white socks."

"But you didn't notice if the rider was an officer?"

"I couldn't tell because I was far away, in the sun, and he was in the thick shade, almost dark."

"Small? Thin?"

"Yes, he looked very thin and small."

There was no doubt. Poor Colonel Abbati! He was coming to the end of the line.

Over coffee, the conversation struck up again. A second lieutenant, a liberal arts student at the University of Rome, recited a satire by Juvenal in Latin and then gave his Italian translation in verse. We all applauded.

"As far as I'm concerned, you could have spared yourself the Latin," said Lieutenant Grisoni. "I studied it for ten years, always first in my class, but I didn't understand a thing of those verses you recited. Not only that, but you pronounce Latin like you had a mouthful of beans."

We were all feeling good. It didn't even seem like we were

under artillery fire. Despite it all, we felt like we could breathe again. It felt like the war was over and forgotten.

The trill of the telephone interrupted the conversation. I got up and went to the phone. The officers fell silent. A senior captain, the regimental adjutant, was asking for me.

"What is it?" I asked.

"You've got to get ready, because tomorrow the regiment is going down."

"For a rest down on the plains?" I asked, pleased.

"No, we're not cut out for rest."

"And where are we going?"

"To the high plateau of Bainsizza. The offensive on that front has started and the brigade has been requested by the army commander in person."

"What an honor!"

"What can you do? Is your battalion ready?"

"Yes, the battalion is ready. But are you really sure we're being sent to the Bainsizza?"

"Yes, I'm sure. I decoded the order myself."

"What time?"

"That will be communicated tomorrow morning, at the battalion commanders' report."

"All right. Good-bye."

"Good-bye."

The officers were holding their breath. They hadn't heard the adjutant's words but they'd understood everything from my responses. Mute, they looked me in the eye with anguish on their faces. The cavalry lieutenant filled his glass and said, "Let's drink to the Bainsizza!"

His colleagues followed suit.

The offensive on the Bainsizza!

The war was starting up again.

AFTERWORD

Mark Thompson

A Soldier on the Southern Front is one of the finest books about the First World War, and the best by an Italian veteran. More than any other, it communicates what we take to have been the essential history and experience of Italian soldiers. It is all here: the unstinting obedience of the infantry, broken by sullen mutinies; the ineffable arrogance of commanding officers, committed to hopeless tactical procedures; the savagery of "military justice," including the unique practice of decimation; the obtuse dogmatism of the staff officers; the warmth of comradeship in the trenches; the drunkenness (for the front was awash with alcohol); the pleasures of leave; the sonorous rhetoric of patriotism and sacrifice; the tragedies of "friendly fire"; the inhuman tension before a frontal attack; even down to details, such as the distribution of cardboard boots to front-line units.

Above all, the book is saturated with a very Italian conviction of the war's immense political significance. Yet the narrative is so dynamic and fresh, never clogged by extraneous information and sometimes lightened by black humor, that we read on for pleasure.

Lussu and the Great War

Emilio Lussu (1890–1975) was a figure of vivid and noble distinction in twentieth-century Italy. As an activist, author, and politician, he worked tirelessly over decades to build, strengthen, and transform democratic governance in his region and his country. He was born in 1890 in a village not far from Cagliari, in southeastern Sardinia. The village was poor, but Lussu's family was not, and after schooling in Rome, Emilio studied law at the university in Cagliari. Sardinia was little affected by the political turbulence that shook the mainland in the first months of 1915, when "interventionists"—who wanted Italy to join the war against Germany and Austria—quarrelled and sometimes fought in the streets with the "neutralists," who wanted Italy to stay aloof from the conflict.

Like thousands of students throughout Italy, Lussu demanded that Italy join the fray alongside Britain, France, and Russia in order to defeat the Central Powers. By driving Austria beyond the Alps, Italy would finally liberate the Habsburg-ruled territories in northeastern Italy. This would complete the patriotic and democratic project of national unification that Garibaldi and Cavour had launched half a century before.

As a reserve officer, Lussu was mobilised in early May 1915, only two weeks after he graduated. He was shipped to the mainland on May 13, as Second Lieutenant with 10th Company, 3rd Battalion, 151st Regiment, in the newly formed Sassari Brigade. Ten days later, Italy was at war.

As part of a nation-building policy, Italian army units were composed of soldiers from different regions. Uniquely among the infantry brigades, the Sassari's six thousand men were recruited from a single region: the island of Sardinia. Perhaps this decision was a practical concession to the dialect of *sardo*, incomprehensible to mainlanders. At some level, anyway, it recognized the strength of Sardinian identity.

The Sassari was formed of agricultural workers, peasants, farmhands, and shepherds, led by reserve officers, most of them also Sardinian. The brigade became known for its iron code of honor, its men's powerful bonds of loyalty and extreme respect for authority, and the fierce rivalry between its two regiments (the 151st and the 152nd). From an early point in the war, a certain rhetoric was used about the Sardinians in official communiqués: intrepid, ferocious, strong sons of Italy, undaunted by bullets, and the like. The brigade saw action from the Carso to the Piave, from summer 1915 to November 1918. Throughout this time, the number of deserters was extremely—perhaps uniquely—low in the Italian army. On Mount Fior, in June 1916, the brigade retreated in the face of the enemy for first time. (Lussu narrates this episode with Homeric simplicity in chapter VI.)

By any standard, Lussu was an outstanding soldier. He led from the front. He was loved by his comrades and his men. He was a superb shot. He was decorated four times for valor; his first citation, in November 1916, stated that "his calm and courage were an example to all." His fourth, in June 1918, hailed him as "always foremost in danger, giving an example of ardor and courage to his men." He seemed charmed, passing unscathed through the worst slaughter. (His only wound, late in the war, was not serious.) Other officers called him "the finest captain in the regiment," a "magnificent commander," the idol of his men. One of these, Nicolò La Rosa, wrote in his diary about Lussu's "habitual calm," that he was unfazed by disaster when given command of a battalion that had been reduced to sixty men. And his courage was more than physical. On at least two occasions, Lussu dared to contradict his superiors—at the risk of summary execution.

On November 4, 1918, he learned about the armistice from a cyclist who was passing the news from divisional headquarters. (His colonel confided glumly, "If the war had lasted another month, I'd have made general.") He was elected unanimously as the first president of the veterans' association in Cagliari in 1919, before he was discharged.

His political career was a result of the Great War. In 1921, Lussu joined other veterans in founding a new political party, which aimed to create a leftist movement and culture in Sardinia. Elected to parliament in Rome, he became a prominent and vocal anti-Fascist, and was targeted accordingly by the regime. When *squadristi* invaded his home in 1926, he shot and killed one of the assailants. Sentenced to prison on the island of Lipari, he escaped to Paris, where he helped to establish the Justice and Liberty (*Giustizia e Libertà*) movement. He also wrote and published several books: a mordant account of Mussolini's seizure of power, a manual of rebellion against tyranny, and *A Soldier on the Southern Front*.

Lussu was active in the Resistance, initially from exile in France and then—from August 1943—back in Italy. After the war, he served as minister of reconstruction in the first peacetime government, then dedicated himself again to the Sardinian scene, and to autonomy and federalism as the right goals of regional (Sardinian) and national (Italian) development. He spent his last years in Rome, always with his wife, Joyce Salvadori Lussu (1912–1998), herself a notable anti-Fascist partisan and translator.

The School of Revolution

Written in 1936 and 1937 while Lussu was convalescing after a serious operation, and published in Paris the following year, *A Soldier on the Southern Front* could not be published in Italy until the summer of 1945, when it drew praise from eminent critics and writers, including Benedetto Croce and Eugenio Montale.[1] It has never subsequently been out of print. This is perhaps more remarkable given that the book's streamlined urgency—what one of its best critics, Simonetta Salvestrini, calls "the sense of rebellion that runs through it from first to last, destroying the most cherished myths and values"—reflects Lussu's embattled but undaunted stance in the European crisis of the mid-1930s. This book was written more as an anti-Fascist intervention than as a pitch at immortality, not because Lussu wished to write a polemic, but because he was the man he was, entirely aware of the mortal threat posed by Fascism to the future of Europe and humankind, and committed to the struggle against that threat.

"If it is waged with open eyes," Lussu wrote elsewhere in 1938, "every war is a school of revolution." Lussu the interventionist went to war in May 1915 with eyes clamped shut. *A Soldier on the Southern Front* does not explain directly how the author's eyes were opened; rather, it sets out the circumstances in which enlightenment was the inevitable result. Indeed, this book is the fruit of that process.

Lussu was convinced that his political awakening in the trenches was a single instance of the wider activation or disillusionment that passed through the Sassari Brigade. For it was an article of faith with him that Sardinian political consciousness was born in the mud and the blood. "Separated for more than a millennium from Italian life," he wrote in an essay in 1938, "Sardinia is nothing other than a historically aborted nation [*una nazione fallita storicamente*]." Living, fighting, and dying with their fellow islanders, however, the men of the Sassari Brigade—removed from their native villages and fields for the first time—discovered what Sardinia was. And this discovery was ineluctably political. "For the first time, the Sardinians realized that war was waged only by the peasants, shepherds and workers. . . . They also concluded that the colonels and generals understood nothing. Certain stupid, outrageous actions revealed that the general was, in reality, the enemy."

This realization was not restricted to the Sardinians. "If the Socialist Party had only grasped that the trenches had taught the peasants what the factories had taught the workers, and that a psychological revolution had taken place," Lussu concluded, "Mussolini would have ended up in prison instead of in power."

Lussu's identity as a Sardinian sharpened the acute contradictions of his situation. An ardent interventionist who had clamored for Italy to join the war, he then spent three and a half years alongside men—his fellow Sardinians—who were fighting and dying for a state that had never shown any interest in them beyond exploitation, in an army that treated them, at least until the end of 1917, as so much cannon fodder, against an enemy who meant nothing to them—for Austria and Germany meant no more to ordinary Sardinians than Russia or Britain.

An episode that must have affected his reeducation was the catastrophe on Mount Zebio in late June and July 1916. Hundreds of soldiers died in attacks against unbroken barbed wire, pouring uphill day after day from trenches that in some places were only a dozen yards from the enemy line (chapters X to XVII). A comrade found Lussu in tears: "Until now I've acted as an officer. But now I'm meant to lead my men to be massacred pointlessly." After twenty days, according to Alfredo Graziani, Lussu refused an order from the divisional commander, on the grounds that another attack would be tantamount to murdering his men.

In short, a political analysis of the war in terms of class and regional hierarchies was forced upon Lussu in the trenches. Yet the Sardinian dimension—central to Lussu's experience—is absent from this book. Why so? Because *A Soldier on the Southern Front* was intended as a national story with universal implications.

Fact and Fiction

Lussu wrote in his preface to the book that it consisted simply of personal memories of a single year of the war, assembled in a somewhat haphazard fashion, with real names altered. This was true. Most of the named individuals in the book are, transparently, versions of real people: Grisoni was Lieutenant Alfredo Graziani, Melchiorri was Major Marchese, Carriera was Lieutenant Colonel Emanuele Pugliese, Santini was Lieutenant Giovanni Santi, Ottolenghi was Lieutenant Nicola Ottaviani, and Canevacci was Captain Carnevali. The monstrous General Leone was very likely based on General Giacinto Ferrero. Leone and his successor, General Piccolomini, incarnate the military establishment's failings; Leone is a portrait of innate stupidity reinforced by a structure that forbade true assessment of performance, while Piccolomini concentrates the shortcomings of the General Staff: pedantic, ignorant, vainglorious. Even the officers and men unnamed by Lussu can sometimes be identified from other sources; the colonel who contradicts General Leone about the efficacy of Farina body armor (chapter XIV) was Stanislao Mammuccari.

Likewise with the events and the chronology. The Sassari Brigade really did transfer from the Isonzo front to the Asiago plateau in spring 1916, and really did fight on the mountains named in Lussu's book. The shooting of Marrasi (chapter XXI) was based on the shooting of infantryman Marras, one of the brigade's few deserters. Scholars who have compared the book point for point with regimental diaries, veterans' memoirs, and other sources have found only minor discrepancies. The mutiny in chapter XXIV happened in January 1916, not in January 1917. The episode in which a cavalry officer is teased about his courage and responds by getting himself killed (chapter XVI) was based on the death of Second Lieutenant Otto Giulini earlier in the war, on the Carso plateau. Farina body armor was not as rare as Lussu makes out (chapter XIV). Other sources paint a slightly less terrible picture of winter conditions in 1916–1917. Or consider the episode where Colonel Carriera insists that Lieutenant Santini carry out an impossible operation that can only lead to his death (chapter XII). In Graziani's account, Santi fired his pistol at the enemy trench from a distance of some ten meters. Lussu's Santini does not shoot; instead, he puts his pistol back in its holster. This sharpens Santi's rebelliousness, underscoring the brutal stupidity of his commanding officer.

In at least one case, Lussu's characterization was colored by postwar events. His harsh treatment of Carriera ("career" in Italian, i.e., careerist) reflected his loathing of Emanuele Pugliese. In October 1922, as the commanding officer in Rome, General Pugliese—the most decorated officer in the army—disobeyed orders to block the Fascist Blackshirts from entering the capital. Lussu never forgave him; in July 1945, two months after the end of the war, he wrote publicly that Pugliese deserved to be shot for his complicity in Mussolini's seizure of power.

The prominence of Ottolenghi in the narrative needs some comment. His rebellious zest permeates the book. His model, Nicola Ottaviani, was a socialist who opposed the war on principle. This made him a very rare bird among the officers of the Sassari Brigade. He may have loomed larger in Lussu's memories than in his life and thoughts at the time. Ottolenghi's role reflects his importance to Lussu and to the lessons that he wanted readers to draw from his book.

It would be absurd, however, to claim that the reader is misled by any of this, or to argue that Lussu should only be trusted historically when he can be corroborated. For *A Soldier on the Southern Front* is an important source in itself. The scene in chapter xv, for example, when an Austrian chaplain tells the Italians to stop attacking ("*Basta! Basta!*"), is not recorded by any other witness. This does not mean it did not happen, for similar episodes were attested elsewhere on the Italian front, and official chroniclers would be reluctant to mention such disgraces.

Style and Ambivalence

Lussu's style is spare, muscular, almost reportorial; the tone is informal, flexible, ironic, humorous, dry, sometimes scathing. It exposed by contrast the lying clichés of official propaganda and the flabbiness of orthodox military thinking. It also subverted the Fascist mythology of the sacred holocaust. For Mussolini's regime had turned the Great War into a foundation myth. The scale of bloodshed—nearly 700,000 dead, another million seriously wounded—was taken as proof of national greatness.

Ossuaries were built around the northeastern border—one of them, at Redipuglia, on a pharaonic scale—to combine the functions of charnel houses and patriotic shrines. Unvarnished accounts of the front such as Lussu's, and honest investigations of Italian strategy and tactics, were censored or suppressed.

The book's corrosive power may be underestimated or even missed by American and British readers today, because our cynicism about the ideals once associated with the Great War is so complete that we can hardly imagine what it would mean to believe or half believe in them, and then lose them. The drama of such disenchantment drives Lussu's book, which traces, obliquely, the author's evolution from callow interventionism to wholesale disillusion with the system of governance—political as much as military—that let Italy wage war with such horrifying incompetence.

This drama is rendered without a hint of confessional pathos. The first-person narration is undecided or open-minded, as if suspending judgment on the horrors that it reports. The narrator is committed to the war, sees everything, can be dismayed but not disheartened. For it is a story of action, not reflection, except in two decisive chapters. In chapter XIX, the narrator deliberates whether or not to kill a young Austrian soldier drinking coffee, happily unaware of danger. His decision marks an inner liberation from ideology: "It was my duty to shoot. . . . And yet I wasn't shooting. . . . I had a man in front of me. A man!"[2]

Yet this does not mean the narrator is aligned with Ottolenghi's and Canevacci's furious (and, of course, treasonable) conviction that their real enemies are their own commanding officers. He cannot quite disown the democratic and patriotic motives that inspired him in 1915. In chapter XXV, Lussu dramatizes the conflict within his own breast in a dialogue between Ottolenghi and "the Commander of 10th Company." Ottolenghi condemns the war as nothing but useless slaughter (*strage inutile*—words that resonated because Pope Benedict XV had famously used them about the war in 1917), and calls for the army to turn around and march on Rome. The other man agrees that Italy's leaders were unprepared for war, but insists that is no reason to stop fighting. Then he falls silent.

Critics have faulted this discussion as improbable and didactic. Lussu always defended it, and indeed it was fundamental to his divided experience of the war and to his educational purpose in this book. He himself had been both Ottolenghi and the company commander. Thanks to Alfredo Graziani's diary, we also know that he had also been both Leone and the sentry who died at his (the general's) order, in one of the book's unforgettable scenes (chapter VII). It turns out that there was a personal reason why Lussu's book is haunted by loophole 14. Early in the war, he had ordered a soldier to look through a loophole that was under enemy fire. The soldier obeyed, and was killed the next instant. Lussu reacted by pushing his own face up to the loophole and keeping it there. (Read that sentence again: it tells you almost all you need to know about Emilio Lussu.) This was appreciated as a proof of his courage and a gesture of respect for his men.

Without its truthful ambivalence, this book would not

be the masterpiece it is. Lussu denies nothing about the war, however damning or redemptive. The glimpse of squirrels playing (chapter IX), the rocket fireworks (chapter XI), the men's contentment between attacks, when they relax and reread their letters from home (chapter XVI): these feature in the book because they featured in the war.

Near the end of his long life, Lussu was taken to watch *Uomini Contro*, Francesco Rosi's film adapted from this book. He objected that it was too grim: "That is not all there is to war. Sometimes we even sang, joked, and dreamed our dreams." This was more than a cavil. If we remove the human dimension from our accounts of war, they become simply monstrous and demoralizing, less able to fortify us in the unceasing campaign for justice and liberty.

Bibliography

Giuseppe Fiori, *Il cavaliere dei Rossomori: Vita di Emilio Lussu* (Turin: Einaudi, 1985).

Emilio Lussu, «*La Brigata Sassari e il Partito Sardo d'Azione,*» *Il Ponte,* 7, 1951.

Paolo Pozzato, ed., *Un Anno sull'Altopiano con i Diavoli Rossi. Storia delle Brigate «Sassari» e «Reggio» nella Grande Guerra* (Udine: Paolo Gaspari, 2006).

Simonetta Salvestroni, *Emilio Lussu Scrittore* (Florence: La Nuova Italia Editrice, 1974).

Giuseppe Sircana, "LUSSU, Emilio," in *Dizionario Biografico degli Italiani,* volume 66 (2007), Treccani.it, available at http://www.treccani.it/enciclopedia/emilio-lussu_(Dizionario-Biografico), accessed September 2013.

Mark Thompson, *The White War: Life and Death on the Italian Front, 1915–1919* (New York: Basic Books, 2009).

Notes

1. The first English translation was published in 1939 as *Sardinian Brigade*—an odd choice of title. The translator, Marion Rawson, was a founder of the Italian Refugees' Relief Committee, set up in London to support anti-Fascist exiles. The book was favorably noticed in *The New York Times,* as was a reprint in 1968.

2. It would be interesting to know if Lussu had read an extraordinary poem by Fausto Maria Martini. Called "Why I Didn't Kill You" and published in the last winter of the war, the poem versified Martini's decision not to kill an Austrian soldier, a terrified boy cowering under his (Martini's) bayonet. "It was not, then, for fear/that I didn't kill you: it was—not to die myself!/Not to die in you: you were my twin,/or seemed so in the twinned trench."

TRANSLATOR'S NOTES

1. Gaetano Salvemini (1853–1957). In the 1920s Salvemini was Chaired Professor of Modern History at the University of Florence but resigned his position rather than take a loyalty oath to the Fascist regime. Forced into exile in Paris, he was a founder of the anti-fascist movement *Giustizia e Libertà*, of which Emilio Lussu was also a leading member. From Paris he moved on to England and then to the United States, where he taught at Harvard and became a citizen in 1940. After WWII he returned to his teaching position in Florence and began his first lecture with the words, "As I was saying . . . ."

2. Lussu has fictionalized the numbers of the regiments here. The Sassari Brigade was actually composed of the 151st and 152nd Infantry Regiments.

3. The Carso (or Karst) is a limestone plateau region extending between southwestern Slovenia and northeastern Italy.

4. *Quel mazzolin' di fiori* is one of the songs made famous by the *Alpini*, the Italian mountain infantry corps, 125,000 of whom were killed in WWI. After the war, veterans ("*veci*") formed choirs in their hometowns and sang about the hardships of what they called "the war of snow and ice." A choral version of the song can be heard at http://www.youtube.com/watch?v=fPaB7vOoBMM.

5. The Asiago plateau, also known as the plateau of the Seven Communes, is an area of about 200 square miles situated in the southern Alps between Trento on the northwest and Vicenza on the south. First settled by Germanic tribes in Roman times, the seven towns located on the plateau formed an autonomous federation in the early 1300s, which lasted

until Napoleon's invasion of Italy in 1796. Asiago is also famous as the setting for novels and stories by Emilio Lussu's friend and fellow writer Mario Rigoni Stern.

6. To allow a soldier to see out of the trench or fire small arms without exposing his head, a loophole could be built into the parapet. A loophole might simply be a gap in the sandbags, or it might be fitted with a steel plate. For a good photo of a loophole in an Italian trench, see http://www.flickr.com/photos/hansderegt/5124063193/.

7. The acronym SIPE indicated the name of the company that produced them: *Società Italiana Produzione Esplosivi.*

8. The Alpini are an elite mountain warfare military corps of the Italian Army. Established in 1872, the Alpini are the oldest active mountain infantry in the world. During World War I the 26 peacetime Alpini battalions were increased by 62 battalions and saw heavy combat all over the alpine arch.

9. A "malga," as Lusso explains in this passage is a grassy, treeless pasture in the Alps where dairy cows are taken to graze in the summer. But the word is also used to refer to the building where the cows' milk is made into cheese. So Malga Lora is the pasture and the Malga is the building or cabin where the cheese is made.

10. Gelignite, or blasting gelatin, an explosive mixture of nitroglycerin, guncotton, wood pulp and potassium nitrate, was invented in 1875 by Alfred Nobel. Tubes or cylinders of gelignite were used by Italian troops to make breaches in the Austrian barbed wire entanglements, but they were seldom successful.

11. Like Casara Zebio, Casara Zebio Pastorile is a malga located slightly higher up on Mount Zebio. Casara Zebio is at altitude 1680 meters and Casara Zebio Pastorile is at 1706 meters. For photos see http://www.caiasiago.it/puntiappoggio/832app.htm#Malga%20Zebio.

12. The tune is "Marechiaro" written in 1895 by the Neapolitan poet Salvatore Di Giacomo. Marechiaro is a seaside neighbornood in the Posillipo area of Naples.

13. The Benaglia was a rodded fragmentation grenade equipped with 3 tin fins to help it fly nose first. Images and details are available at http://www.talpo.it/benaglia.html.